THE WORLD'S MOST
BAFFLING
UNSOLVED
CRIMES

THE WORLD'S MOST BAFFLING

UNSOLVED CRIMES

BY

NIGEL BLUNDELL

SUNBURST BOOKS

PHOTOGRAPHY CREDITS

Topham: 26, 54.
Hulton Deutsch Collection: 136.

Every effort has been made to trace the ownership of all copyright material
and to secure permission from copyright holders. In the event of any question arising as to the use of any material we will be pleased to make the
necessary corrections in future printings.

This edition published 1996 by Sunburst Books,
Kiln House, 210 New Kings Road,
London SW6 4NZ

ISBN 1 85778 157 0

Printed and bound in Great Britain

Contents

INTRODUCTION

There's nothing like a whodunit to grip the reader. As Agatha Christie discovered, criminal mysteries never fail to fascinate.

But the best thrillers of all are not those dreamt up in the imagination of a crime writer; they are the TRUE tales of mayhem, murder and mystery.

Crime has led men and women to perform amazing feats of duplicity and to create puzzles that defy solutions.

Who, for instance, was the killer they called Jack the Ripper? How did the British royal family become involved in a gangland slaying? Who really assassinated John F Kennedy? And what was the horrific fate of Teamsters' leader Jimmy Hoffa?

Despite the efforts of the agencies of law and order, some of the most celebrated crimes remain unsolved and the perpetrators unpunished.

Here we examine 24 such cases. You will be witness to the fascinating and sometimes gruesome facts that confound the police and keep a crime in the file marked UNSOLVED.

JIMMY HOFFA

Jimmy Hoffa was the 'biggest little guy in the USA'. His firebrand exploits were the stuff of legend, lovingly reported by the media. He was that curiously American animal – a tainted folk hero. His mysterious disappearance in 1975 has intrigued the public and confounded the authorities. There have been umpteen conflicting theories of his fate, but nothing concrete – not even a 'cement overcoat'.

The reason for the fascination in his fate is not hard to fathom. Hoffa, a trade union bigshot, had fought the Kennedys, courted the Mafia, stolen workers' millions, been imprisoned, courted Richard Nixon, done battle with the Mafia, won back the workers and split the unions – and then he was suddenly gone.

So what happened? Was he turned into glue? Ground up in a mincer? Compacted in a garbage plant? Cemented into a bridge? Squashed inside a junked car? Fed to Florida's alligators? Or could he perhaps still be alive?

The day he vanished, all of America knew instantly that foul play was afoot. There was no question: Jimmy Hoffa, pint-sized firebrand, former jailbird and one of the nation's prominent labour leaders, had surely been murdered. He'd had it coming to him after all.

The aptly named James Riddle Hoffa was born in poverty on 14 February 1913. In the tough Depression Era, he worked his way up from a docker's job to become president of the United States' largest and most powerful trade union, the International Brotherhood of Teamsters. Anything that moved around the US, by truck, ship or rail, involved this union. And anything that involved the union also involved the Mafia.

Under the direction of Hoffa from his Detroit headquarters, the Teamsters changed from being a disorganised rabble into a major force. Even the Michigan State Police joined Hoffa's union. All employees and employers alike paid into the enormous Teamsters' pension fund, which was mercilessly milked by Hoffa's mob supporters. Attorney General Robert Kennedy pursued Hoffa and his fellow officials with a vengeance, but he was never able to nail him for the web of fraud he had spun.

Hoffa had been arrested 23 times, but somehow no significant charges ever stuck. The 5ft 5in/1.6m firebrand boasted that he had 'a record as long as your arm', but in fact he had been fined only twice – a paltry $10 and $1,000 – and had never been to jail.

Hoffa's luck finally began to run out in 1964 when he received an eight-year sentence for jury tampering. That same year he was given an additional five-year sentence for defrauding the Teamsters' pension fund of $2 million. A string of appeals failed and he went to prison in 1967.

Teamsters' union president Jimmy Hoffa was
constantly followed by the media, who voraciously
reported his firebrand exploits which were not loved
by all – especially the Mafia.

Astonishingly, for a cheat who had stolen their hard-earned funds, Hoffa was still a hero with his fanatically loyal union members. And from inside prison he continued to influence the union's affairs. Hoffa had planned for a weak 'caretaker', his Detroit deputy Frank Fitzsimmons, to head the Teamsters while he was in jail. Fitzsimmons, however, wanted power in his own right. He failed to follow the strict orders relayed to him from inside the prison cell. Hoffa seethed.

In December 1971, after his parole appeal had been rejected for the third time, Hoffa was suddenly freed – his sentence astonishingly commuted by President Richard Nixon. The union boss had served only 58 months of his 13-year sentence. There was a catch to the Nixon deal, however, in that Hoffa was barred from union activities until 1980. This date just happened to coincide with the end of Fitzsimmons' term of office.

Despite being freed from jail on the president's direct orders, Hoffa complained publicly that Nixon had conspired with Fitzsimmons to betray him. Hoffa was particularly upset because he had promised Nixon the endorsement of the Teamsters and other unions in his 1972 election.

But why would the president get involved at all? For money, said the Phoenix-based *Arizona Republic* newspaper, which in 1979 published the diary of Mafia paymaster Edward 'Marty' Buccieri who was murdered in 1975. The diary, handed to the FBI by convicted hitman Gerald Denono, itemised $28 million of illegal financial transactions in a 15-month period between 1972 and 1973. The diary names Nixon aides Bob Haldeman, Charles Colson and John Ehrlichman, and catalogues half a million dollars of Mafia funds going directly to the president of the United States.

Out of prison, Hoffa desperately tried to wrest control of the Teamsters away from Frank Fitzsimmons. He told his old supporters: 'I know the union business upside down around and over. The members are interested in how many bucks they can make. I get them for them.'

Where persuasion failed, violence began to have an effect. The union was torn apart by civil war. The Teamsters' Detroit office was machine-gunned, an official's boat was blown up, another official was blinded by a shotgun, other union activists were beaten up and the union-owned car of Fitzsimmons' son Dickie, a local branch official, was dynamited.

Although Dickie Fitzsimmons survived, because he had stopped for a drink in a bar, the attack was obviously the last straw for the anti-Hoffa forces. On 30 July 1975, exactly three weeks after the bomb attack, Jimmy Hoffa vanished.

That evening, 62-year-old Hoffa took a phone call and told his wife Josephine that he was going out. He drove from his suburban home in Lake Orion, 45 miles north of Detroit, to the Machus Red Fox restaurant in Bloomfield Township. There he had a dinner date with two Mafia hoodlums – Anthony Giacolone and Anthony Provenzano, better known as Tony Pro. Neither of them turned up at the restaurant – but Hoffa did, and was abducted somewhere in the street outside.

One witness saw him in what may have been the last moments of his life. By chance the witness drew up alongside a brand new maroon Mercury car outside the Machus Red Fox restaurant and for a few seconds saw what everyone believes was the abduction. He recognised Hoffa as one of the four passengers. He was leaning forward shouting at the driver and he had his hands behind his back.

The witness identified the driver from mugshot files as being Charles 'Chuckie' O'Brien, Hoffa's own foster son. Raised by Hoffa, Chuckie became his bodyguard and personal assistant. Hauled in by police, he vehemently proclaimed his innocence. The maroon Mercury was, however, tracked down by the FBI. Sniffer dogs picked up Hoffa's scent on the back seat – and in the trunk.

Both Giacolone and Provenzano made sure they had alibis for the night in question. Indeed, Tony Pro was conspicuously at his home in New Jersey the day he was supposed to be meeting Hoffa for dinner.

Giacolone was a simple Detroit hood. But Provenzano, a former amateur boxer, was a member of the influential Mafia crime family of Vito Genovese – and a local leader of the Teamsters in Union City, New Jersey. Hoffa and Tony Pro bore a fierce hatred for one another. They had been friends and allies, but during a stay they shared at the federal penitentiary in Lewisburg, PA, they fell out. Although Tony Pro almost certainly knew Hoffa's fate, the decision to act must have come from a much higher authority.

Mafia boss Russell Bufalino is reputed to have ordered Hoffa's death. The accepted theory is that the Mob's operation to extort money from employers and to siphon off the union's pension funds was working so effectively under Fitzsimmons that they didn't want Hoffa returning to ruin it all.

After his abduction, the FBI launched the biggest manhunt in its history and continued to keep open the file on Hoffa's disappearance. But not a single arrest was ever made and no evidence was ever found of Hoffa's body.

Was Provenzano the master hitman? We shall never know. Two years after Hoffa's disappearance, Provenzano was given a life sentence for the murder of another Teamsters' official. In 1988 he died in prison aged 71.

Did Fitzsimmons order the killing, as one US government report has claimed? Twice in the year before his death, Hoffa had sent emissaries to the Justice Department offering evidence against his opponent. It's a theory no one can back up. Lung cancer killed Fitzsimmons in the summer of 1981, terminating his Teamsters' presidency.

Or, most extraordinarily of all, was the CIA behind the crime? Through Hoffa, the agency had recruited Mafia bosses Sam Giancana and John Roselli to assassinate Cuba's Fidel Castro. Both Roselli and Giancana were later murdered and their killers never found.

Eerily, Hoffa may have known that he was to be the target of a hit. Just before he vanished, he drew out a million dollars in cash. Although this raised speculation that he might still be alive and on the run, his family remained convinced that he was murdered. His wife died in 1980 after a long illness. His children, James and Barbara continued, for some time, to fight to have the FBI release files that could finally provide the answer to one of the most mysterious unsolved crimes of all time.

SIR HARRY OAKES

Edward VIII of England was a blot on the royal landscape. Assuming the throne on the death of his father George V in January 1936, he insisted on choosing as his queen the beautiful American divorcée Wallis Simpson. Within 12 months of his liaison with Mrs Simpson, he had been forced to abdicate, then went into exile, looking a fool.

As Nazi war clouds loomed, one of the most irritating dilemmas facing the British government was what to do with the ex-king, now titled Duke of Windsor. As long as he remained in Europe, his Nazi sympathies made him an embarrassment to the throne. Prime Minister Winston Churchill came up with the brilliant brainwave of conveniently shipping him off to the colonies.

In 1941 the duke and Wallis, now his wife, finally sailed from neutral Portugal on the Canadian ship *Lady Somers* bound for the Bahamas. But blundering Edward could not be kept out of trouble even in that far, peaceful outpost of the empire. His shadowy dealings in the colony were later to force a split with Britain forever.

American authorities already had the duke down as a Nazi sympathiser and his wife as being on Hitler's payroll, so a careful watch was being kept upon the unlikely ambassadors. The United States became increasingly alarmed, however, when the Windsors became an unwitting tool of the Mafia.

Enter the notorious gangster Meyer Lansky. A murderer and high-ranking Mafia godfather, he was one of the original cast of Murder Incorporated, which had claimed an estimated 800 lives. Lansky teamed up with Bahamian lawyer Stafford Sands and property dealer Harold Christie in a bid to bring gambling to the Bahamas. Their first stroke of luck came within months when Sands was appointed legal adviser to the government and quickly started moves towards legalisation.

Christie introduced the Duke of Windsor to Meyer Lansky in Palm Beach, Florida, and the former British king lent his weight to the prospect of a Riviera-style casino in the colony's capital, Nassau. There was a hitch, however. One of the islands' richest men, 68-year-old Sir Harry Oakes, tried to stall the plans because he could not bear the thought of more wealthy tourists shattering the tranquillity of the islands he so loved.

The duplicitous Sands knew that Sir Harry was determined the idea should not get off the ground, but he had also appraised how desperate Lansky was to get the project started. In May 1943 Lansky offered Sands a $1 million backhander if gambling were legalised in the colony.

At 7am on 8 July 1943 Sir Harry Oakes was murdered and his body set alight in his bed at his ocean-front mansion, Westbourne. Curiously, the fire

Sir Harry Oakes (right), who fought the Mafia and
Harold Christie (left) to stop gambling from entering
Bermuda, met a violent death at his ocean-front
mansion. Christie was the only other person in the
house at the time.

did not spread, save to char the bedclothes and mosquito netting. Apart from the victim, Christie was the only other person in the house at the time.

It was at this point that the Duke of Windsor, as governor, intervened in the most unseemly and suspicious manner. For no obvious reason, he used wartime emergency powers to ban press reports of the death. Then he decided to take personal charge of the murder inquiry.

The duke could have asked local police to help him. On hand beyond them was the FBI in the United States, while detachments of Scotland Yard men could have been drafted in from Washington or New York. Instead, the duke telephoned Miami police headquarters and asked for one Captain James Barker, whom it is possible, though unlikely, he had met before. Could the duke have known that Barker was a Lansky man, bought and paid for by the Mafia and who had once tried to entice his entire police department into a deal with the Mafia?

The duke visited the scene of the crime later the same day and was told that Sir Harry's son-in-law was the prime suspect. Sir Harry had hated his daughter's husband, Count Freddie de Marigny, believing him to be a gold digger. Within hours, 33-year-old de Marigny was charged and thrown into jail. The penalty he faced was death by hanging – and it was a fate he almost met through an appalling miscarriage of justice.

Witnesses rolled up to tell the court how much de

Marigny hated his father-in-law. The court was agog to hear police claims that there had been a violent bust-up between Oakes and de Marigny, and that their suspect had been in the area on the night of the murder. Details of de Marigny's failing finances certainly pointed to a motive. But the clinching details were fingerprint evidence, taken from a Chinese screen beside Oakes's bed, and a singed hair on de Marigny's forearm.

The defence produced their own witnesses who had seen de Marigny burn himself trying to light a candle. Then a fingerprint expert from New Orleans proved that the police print could not have been taken from a rough surface like the etched screen, but must have come from a flat surface such as a glass. The prosecution case was suddenly in tatters and appeared to have been fabricated from start to finish.

As the trial got underway, the Duke and Duchess of Windsor had begun a seven-week holiday in Miami. There was apparently no question of the duke remaining to give his version of events.

At one dramatic point in the trial, defence lawyer Godfrey Higgs asked Captain Barker: 'May I suggest that your desire for personal gain has caused you to sweep aside the truth and fabricate the evidence?'

Barker: 'No sir.'

Higgs: 'Did not His Royal Highness the governor visit you at Westbourne and come to Sir Harry's room at the time you were processing fingerprints?'

Barker: 'He did.'

Higgs: 'I don't think it would be proper for me to inquire as to why he came or what was said.'

Chief Justice Sir Oscar Daly, who presided at the trial, fiercely attacked Barker for the dubious quality of the prosecution case. De Marigny was acquitted, but no thanks to the duke of Windsor, who might have left an innocent man to hang while he sunned himself in Miami.

It was never explained what had transpired between the duke and Barker while the policeman fabricated the evidence. Not even the judge pressed for the truth. It could only be speculation as to whether the duke was lured into Mafia deals with the promise of a payout at the end. Had he allowed himself to be shamelessly used by the ruthless, greedy and scheming?

The duke and duchess, who had always loathed their exile in the Bahamas, escaped to the US as often as possible. A disturbing pointer to the duke's dubious business dealings there came to light in a US intelligence report in May 1943. It read ominously: 'The Duke of Windsor has been finding many excuses to attend private business meetings in the United States, which he is doing at present.'

The Duke of Windsor finally resigned his position and left the island in March 1945. Meanwhile, Lansky and Sands continued in their efforts to bring gambling to the islands.

While the Mafia gangs concentrated on their interests in Cuba, Sands again produced an application for a casino licence. This time he claimed that a British syndicate of businessmen was behind the venture and that the members included Viscount Camrose and earls Dudley, Derby and Sefton. All were friends of the duke of Windsor. According to Lord Derby, however, they knew nothing about the syndicate or its application. On this occasion, the duke of Windsor himself wisely refused to become involved, despite approaches from Harold Christie. The application was refused.

Repercussions from the murder still had Bahamian society trembling. Sixteen years on, the leader of the black Progressive Liberal party and editor of the *Bahamian Times*, Cyril Stevenson, pushed for an inquiry. He said: 'This whole business has been one big whitewash from start to finish. People in high places know who the killer is. It is time the true facts were brought out into the open so that the nightmare of violence this colony has suffered be ended.'

He was referring, of course, to Meyer Lansky, aided and abetted by Harold Christie. Yet despite a vote in the Bahamian House of Assembly to call in Scotland Yard, the facts remained clouded in mystery. For, as they flew to Nassau, there was more double-dealing. As soon as they landed, the British police were sent home. The governor of the day, Sir Oswald Raynor Arthur, declared: 'There will be no new inquiry. The case is closed.'

The Mafia finally had its way and made the Bahamian casinos their own.

And what of the other curious players in this tawdry affair?

Captain James Barker of the Miami police, the cop strangely called in to investigate Harry Oakes's murder, became a hopeless junkie on drugs supplied to him by his Mafia paymasters. He was eventually shot dead by his own son, who was acquitted of murder on the grounds of justifiable homicide.

Bahamian businessman Harold Christie remained in Nassau, a rich and respected member of the community, until his death there in 1973. In 1964 he had been knighted 'for services to the crown' by the Duke of Windsor's niece, Queen Elizabeth II.

And the Duke of Windsor? After leaving the island in 1945, he and Wallis continued their lifelong exile in Paris, until his death at the age of 78 in 1972 and hers at the age of 90 in 1986.

WILLIAM
DESMOND TAYLOR

When police arrived at the smart Los Angeles town house, they expected to be investigating a case of natural death. Instead, they chanced upon one of the most bizarre murder cover-ups of all time. The place was buzzing with activity. Hollywood studio executives raced around, emptying closets and drawers. Papers were being burned in the fireplace and in the midst of this chaos lay a body.

The body in Bungalow 404 of the Alvarado Court complex, in the city's Westlake district, belonged to famed movie director William Desmond Taylor. He lay serenely on the floor, a smile on his lips, a diamond ring on his finger and a bullet in his back. Although a chair lay tipped over beside him, his clothes were perfectly arranged and a monogrammed handkerchief lay alongside him. He looked for all the world as if he had composed himself for a peaceful afternoon nap.

Among those busying themselves around the corpse were two top executives of Paramount Pictures and one of the studio's young comediennes, Mabel Normand. They were trashing documents, burning papers and rummaging through drawers. Incongruously, Taylor's black valet Henry Peavey, who had actually discovered the body, studiously and eerily washed up the previous night's dirty dishes in the kitchen.

As the cops began their investigation that sunny morning of 2 February 1922, Los Angeles finest were utterly confounded. It was only as they cleared the 11 scampering studio staff from the house that they realised a blatant attempt at a cover-up had been made. The movie men were not trying to disguise the fact that a murder had taken place; that would have been impossible. They were attempting to sanitise the house to avoid a scandal – to hide the fact that the dead man was bisexual.

They failed. For this case became a whodunit of epic Hollywood proportions. It had every ingredient beloved of the salacious screen and the scandal-mongering press. There was a handsome hero, a sultry starlet, an evil stage mother, drugs, scandal and lots of sex. It was an unfortunate end to the glittering career of one of the infant film industry's most respected names.

William Desmond Taylor was born plain William Cunningham Deane-Tanner on 26 April 1872 to a middle-class Anglo-Irish family living in County Waterford. At the age of 18, the rebellious William ran away from his Irish home to join an English theatre company. When that did not work out, he emigrated to America and took jobs from waiter and railroad worker to travelling salesman.

At the age of 23, William again took to the stage,

It took years for William Desmond Taylor to reach the fame he always wanted, but this was finally achieved when he directed *Anne of Green Gables*. It all ended tragically though, with a bullet in his back.

this time in New York. There a Broadway chorus girl fell for him, married him and introduced him to her rich parents – who set him up in an antique business. The Deane-Tanners appeared happy for seven years, during which time a daughter was born. But in 1908, bored and dissatisfied with his suburban life, William took some money out of their business account, went on a fierce bender and absconded.

He worked on the stage in New Jersey and Hawaii, in a Canadian paper mill and for a Yukon gold mining company before ending up in Hollywood in 1912. By now he had changed his name to William Desmond Taylor, although the reason for such a choice has never been recorded. At the age of 40, Taylor had at last found his spiritual home.

For two years Taylor played successfully in a string of silent adventure films before being allowed to direct a movie for the very first time. Just as finding Hollywood gave Taylor a home, in directing he found his true vocation. He also found a new love, actress Neva Gerber, and they became engaged.

Both Taylor's romance and his career were halted by the First World War. In 1918 he did his duty by joining the British Army, was posted to Canada and eventually called to England, where he was made an officer. The war ended before he saw action, however, and he returned to Hollywood and to Paramount Pictures for whom he directed the classic *Anne of Green Gables* starring a naive 17-year-old named Mary Miles Minter.

Mary fell desperately in love with the 47-year-old director. But, almost in a Hollywood cliché, Mary had a pushy mother, Charlotte Shelby, who was also her agent. This woman, fiercely ambitious for her daughter, was anxious to keep her influence over her – as well as keep control of her income. Mother barred Mary from seeing Taylor.

The impressionable girl survived the ban by penning girlish fantasies to the director. 'I'd go to my room and put on something scant and flowing,' she wrote in one letter. 'Then I would lie on the couch and wait for you. I might fall asleep, for a fire makes me drowsy. Then I'd wake to find two strong arms around me and two sweet lips pressing on mine in a long sweet kiss.'

Although there is no evidence that Taylor had a sexual affair with Mary, her mother accused the director of leading the girl astray. It is likely that the ambitious matriarch, a failed actress herself, had her own heart set on Taylor and was jealous of her daughter's success. Shelby once visited Taylor's bungalow in Alvarado Court, believing her daughter was there. Taylor allowed her to search the building. She found nothing – but later claimed that if she had, she would have used the .38 revolver hidden beneath her coat. On another occasion, Mary Miles Minter returned to her mother's home and was accused of having been with Taylor. After Shelby threw a glass of water over her daughter, the girl screamed: 'I'm going to end it all.' She locked herself in a bedroom and fired off several shots from a pistol – but only into the ceiling, walls and floor.

Was either of these gun-slinging females the killer of William Desmond Taylor? Or was it another girl who had come into his life – Mabel Normand?

Mabel was Hollywood's top comedienne at the age of 22. She starred in many of Mack Sennett's Keystone comedies – as well as appearing regularly in his bed. When their romance ended in acrimony because of Sennett's womanising, Mabel turned to drink and drugs. By the time she and Taylor began seeing one another in 1920, Mabel was a cocaine addict. Mabel Normand, it was later revealed, had visited Taylor's bungalow on the night before his body was found. And her presence there the following day was to remove letters that she had written to him 'to prevent terms of affection being misconstrued'.

William Taylor was fiercely opposed to the growing use of drugs in Hollywood. He is known to have had a violent row with Mabel's pusher. Was it this unknown person who pulled the trigger of the gun that killed Taylor?

Or was there a more sinister reason for his death? For it was rumoured that William Desmond Taylor enjoyed the favours of men as much as he did women. In the days following his death, Hollywood was rife with rumours about piles of pornography and wardrobes of kinky underwear being removed from his home.

One of the first murder suspects was valet Henry

Peavey, the homosexual valet who said he had discovered the body on the morning of 2 February. Only a few months before he had been arrested and charged with soliciting young boys in a nearby park.

Another suspect was a mystery man calling himself Edward F Sands, who had been hired by Taylor as his secretary the previous year. Sands vanished with $4,000 and his boss's sports car. The car was found but the absconder never was.

One of the most remarkable elements of the Taylor murder was that the killer had almost certainly been seen by a neighbour immediately after he had committed the crime.

On the evening of 1 February, Mrs Faith MacLean, heard what sounded like a gunshot and opened the door of her bungalow. The scene was calm and she put the sound down to a car backfiring. Then she noticed a figure emerging from William Taylor's bungalow. 'It was dressed like a man, but funny looking,' she told police. 'And it walked like a woman – quick little steps and short legs.'

In the year following the director's death, police drew up a list of 200 suspects, from homosexuals to husbands of Taylor's supposed mistresses. No one was ever brought to court. According to frustrated Los Angeles detectives, the firmest clue to the identity of the murderer was a nightgown they found in a closet at Bungalow 404 Alvarado Court. It bore the monogram 'MMM'.

Whichever of the principal suspects murdered

William Desmond Taylor, it is unlikely that the killer lived happily ever after...

The mysterious Sands was found floating in a river, having shot himself through the head, only a few weeks after Taylor's death.

Mabel Normand died of tuberculosis and drug addiction in 1930 at the age of 37.

Taylor's valet, Henry Peavey, died in a ghetto flophouse in 1937.

Evil Charlotte Shelby, pursued by daughter Mary in a series of lawsuits over her money, died in a humble Santa Monica home in 1957 at the age of 85.

Mary Miles Minter, shunned by the studios, died an obese, half-crazed hermit in 1984.

Why were none of these ever charged? Byron Fitts, the last surviving LA district attorney who could answer this question, shot himself with a .38 revolver in 1973.

MAN IN THE IRON MASK

He is one of history's most famous prisoners. He was thrown into jail on the direct orders of the Sun King Louis XIV. For 30 years he suffered a prison existence of unremitting hell. When he died, all trace of him was obliterated. Then the poor wretch finally became immortalised by the novelist Alexandre Dumas, as the Man in the Iron Mask.

Who was he? Why was he imprisoned so long? And was his crime so heinous that it warranted the attention of the monarch and the lifelong penalty he was made to pay?

The mask which the unfortunate prisoner was doomed to wear for over three decades was moulded to fit closely to his face. The panels were riveted to foil any attempt at its removal. He ate with it on and slept with it on. The jaw piece was fitted with springs to allow movement for eating and for speaking. But the wearer was threatened with instant death if he ever breathed a word of his true identity, or mentioned the reason for his strange incarceration.

Stories about the Man in the Iron Mask abounded in France before the revolution. It was well known that the celebrated convict was kept prisoner on the orders of Louis XIV. Neither was it a secret that the extravagant ruler, who built the magnificent palace of

Versailles, had ordered the prisoner's identity to be kept a secret.

What made his case even more mysterious, however, was the fact that, although his crime must have been serious indeed, it was seemingly not heinous enough to incur execution. Did he have noble blood in his veins that even the Sun King dared not spill? In support of such rumours was the fact that the captive was permitted certain privileges. He was allowed to attend mass without hindrance, was given books and fine food and allowed luxuries not normally granted to prisoners in the Bastille.

None of the correspondence between prison officials and court functionaries known at that time ever referred to his real identity, but there were some fantastic theories about who he really was...

According to one, he was the twin brother of Louis XIV, and was locked away by the monarch because, in his vanity, he wished to preserve all the glory and privilege of the throne for himself alone.

According to another theory, he was an illegitimate son of the king, conceived after a secret liaison with a farm girl. It was said that his appearance so closely matched the king's that he could never be allowed to be seen in public.

It was not until the Man in the Iron Mask died in the Bastille in 1703 that gossip and public intrigue began to chip away at the wall of secrecy which surrounded him. In 1753, a full 50 years after his ignoble end, a private journal of Etienne du Jonca, the

There has been much speculation about the true identity of the Man in the Iron Mask (top). The truth was never revealed – not even on his burial certificate (bottom), on which a false name was recorded.

king's lieutenant in the jail at the time of his imprisonment, came to light.

For the first time, a document penned by someone in authority actually mentioned the strange, masked prisoner. It announced his arrival at the Bastille in 1698, when he had already spent nearly 30 years behind bars at other prisons. Throughout his incarceration he had always been in the custody of the same governor – the only man, it was later learned, who was ever allowed to see him unmasked. The journal read: 'Thursday 18 September at three o'clock, M de Saint-Mars, governor of the château of the Bastille, made his appearance, coming from the command of the Iles-Sainte-Marguerite-Pignerol, and bringing with him the prisoner whom he caused always to be masked, whose name is not mentioned.'

Five years after that entry, du Jonca records the death of the unknown prisoner and testifies to the use of a black velvet mask. However, historians believe this may have been merely a belated stab at decency by the authorities, who could have removed the iron contraption shortly after his death and fitted a loose cloth one in its place.

Few other descriptions of the captive exist, but one which has survived demonstrates the lengths to which the authorities were prepared to go to preserve the secret of his true identity.

When de Saint-Mars was bringing his important prisoner from St Marguerite in the bay of Cannes up to the Bastille in Paris, they stopped to dine at de

Saint-Mars's château near Villeneuve. Peasants who glanced through the windows of the château noticed that next to de Saint-Mars's plates were loaded pistols, ready to be aimed at his charge should he attempt to reveal his face to the domestic staff.

De Saint-Mars was privileged indeed to have been entrusted with the secret of the identity of the Man in the Iron Mask. For even within the Bourbon royal family, only Louis XV came to know the secret. He is alleged to have said, on hearing who the man was: 'If he were still alive, I would give him his freedom.'

The information was never confided to Louis XVI, who began a fruitless search to discover it, largely to satisfy the curiosity of his truculent and eccentric wife, Marie Antoinette.

It was only with the overthrow of the monarchy during the French Revolution in 1789 that the first real clues as to the man's true identity began to emerge. When state files were plundered, it came to light in the records of the Minister of War, a man called Louvois, that a large number of letters had passed between him and de Saint-Mars concerning the mystery man. At the end of July 1669, the year in which the Man in the Iron Mask was first imprisoned, Louvois wrote to the prison governor:

'The king has commanded that I am to have the man named Eustache Dauger sent to Pignerol. It is of the utmost importance to his service that he should be most securely guarded and that he should in no way give information about himself nor send letters to anyone at all. You will yourself once a day have to take enough food for the day to this wretch and you must on no account listen for any reason at all to what he may want to say to you, always threatening to kill him if he opens his mouth to speak of anything but his necessities.'

Another letter, from the king himself to de Saint-Mars, survived in the archives, and reads:

'I am sending to my citadel of Pignerol, in the charge of Captain de Vauroy, sergeant major of my city and citadel of Dunkirk, the man named Eustache Dauger. You are to hold him in good and safe custody, preventing him from communicating with anyone at all by word of mouth or writ of hand.'

Was Eustache Dauger the Man in the Iron Mask? If he was, how could he possibly be so dangerous to the king of France that he was locked away, forced to suffer the unbearable indignity of having his face encased in iron, and forbidden to communicate his identity on pain of death?

Later research has proved that Eustache Dauger came from a large family and had five sisters and six brothers, four of whom were killed in battle, and was a native of the northern French port of Dunkirk. But why the incarceration?

Some historians believe that Dauger's one surviving brother was made a marquis, enabling Dauger to mingle with the nobility. He may have been introduced to Louis XIV at court. At the age of 22, while serving as a lieutenant in the King's Guards, he was caught celebrating a black mass – a blasphemous travesty of the Christian Mass. It is also widely believed that the person with whom he was involved in devil worship was none other than Madame de Montespan – the king's mistress.

There are two theories to explain the king's action in locking up Dauger. One is that he was protecting his mistress's reputation by removing Dauger to a safe place where he could not start malicious rumours about her bent for practising the black arts. The other theory is that the king was inflamed by a terrible fit of jealousy.

However, if either of these theories is true, why did Louis XIV not kill Dauger? To offend the Sun King's sensibilities was crime enough to warrant an early death. Perhaps Louis wished to wreak an even greater vengeance by keeping him locked up all his life and forcing him to wear the terrible mask.

For even in death, the grotesque apparatus stayed on his face. The Man in the Iron Mask died in one of the countless cells of France's most infamous jail, the Bastille, in 1703. Immediately, his body was removed, his clothes were flung into a furnace, the ironwork in his cell was melted down and the scant furniture was burned. Even the whitewash was removed in case he had tried to leave a pitiful message revealing his true self. Only then was the poor wretch laid to rest in an unmarked grave. It was as if he had never existed.

OSCAR SLATER: CONAN DOYLE'S CASE

Sir Arthur Conan Doyle gave to the world its greatest fictional detective. Greater than Poirot, greater than Maigret, the noble character of Sherlock Holmes is loved and revered around the world and enjoys a following which has long since reached cult status.

The popular image of Holmes is of a wealthy, caped crime fighter who wears a deerstalker hat and who is ably assisted by his friend Watson. But what Conan Doyle imparted to crime fiction was a cool, calculating, skilled brain. And if the maxim is true that every writer gives of himself to his work, Conan Doyle must have been blessed with the qualities with which he endowed Sherlock Holmes.

When it came to a murder most foul in real life, Conan Doyle assumed the persona of his fictional character, and his meticulous investigation helped free a man from an unjust sentence of life imprisonment.

The saga began with the murder of an elderly woman whose personal papers were rifled and a cheap brooch stolen. Miss Marion Gilchrist was murdered in her home in Queen's Terrace, West Prince's Street, Glasgow, on 21 December 1908. The spinster, aged 82, was a virtual recluse whose only real

If Sir Arthur Conan Doyle, creator of Sherlock Holmes had not persisted, Oscar Slater (above) would surely have died in his prison cell, wrongly convicted of the murder of Miss Gilchrist.

link with the outside world was a young maidservant called Helen Lambie, aged 21. It was Helen who would know of the few relatives and friends that came to visit her.

On the night that Miss Gilchrist was murdered, Helen left the house at 7pm to buy the evening newspaper. Her mistress stayed inside, locked behind the double doors of her residence. The outer door was on a latch which could be opened by a piece of string attached to it, running up into Miss Gilchrist's apartment. She would look out of the window if someone came to call and, if she recognised them, admit them by pulling on the string.

Several minutes after Helen's departure, downstairs neighbour Arthur Adams heard the sound of what he thought was a heavy fall coming from Miss Gilchrist's apartment upstairs. He saw that the outer door was open but the door to her apartment remained shut and double locked. He yelled for the old woman but got no answer.

Helen returned moments later and when the door was unlocked a man suddenly rushed out, tearing past them and into the street. Once inside, they found the brutally beaten body of Miss Gilchrist in the dining room. Oddly, the thief had not taken her precious jewel collection, valued over £3,000.

What happened after that becomes confused in deceit, cover-up and the police's need to make a quick arrest. Adams went to get a policeman while Helen ran to the home of Miss Gilchrist's niece, Mrs

Margaret Birrell. She blurted out to her that she had recognised the killer. Mrs Birrell seemed enraged at the maid's suggestion, and told her furiously to keep quiet 'for the sake of the man's reputation'.

There was a furious public reaction to the death of the old spinster. Policemen tracked down a German-born gems dealer called Oscar Slater to New York, where he had travelled on the liner *Lusitania* with his French mistress, both of them using assumed names. The police had evidence that Slater had pawned a cheap brooch of approximately the value of the one taken from Miss Gilchrist's home on the night of the murder. With that slender evidence – and some pretty dubious eyewitness reports stating that he was the man – Oscar Slater was condemned to death.

Slater, who was Jewish, was to spend three weeks in the condemned cell after he was found guilty of the murder before the sentence was commuted to life imprisonment. There the matter might have rested, and Slater would have ended his days in tough penal servitude had it not been for Sir Arthur Conan Doyle.

Conan Doyle read of the trial in a legal work entitled *Famous Scottish Trials*, which outlined the case against Slater and the prosecution evidence. In Conan Doyle's own words: 'To say that the evidence against him was thin was an understatement of the first magnitude.'

With analytical precision worthy of Sherlock Holmes, Conan Doyle punched four gaping holes in the prosecution's case.

First, the brooch which initially heaped suspicion on Slater had been pawned three weeks before the killing had taken place.

Second, Slater had only used an assumed name to flee with his mistress to escape from his wife.

Third, the evidence of the eyewitnesses was discredited because their descriptions of him conflicted. Some said he was clean shaven, others said he was bearded.

And finally, on none of the clothes which Slater had packed for his escape was any blood discovered. It had been a particularly brutal murder, and experts concurred with the writer-turned-detective that there would have been blood on the killer.

Conan Doyle concluded that the unfortunate Slater had been found guilty because the straight-laced, puritanical, Scottish jury had been swayed by the prosecution portrayal of him as an amoral, gambling womaniser.

Conan Doyle put all his arguments in a book entitled *The Case of Oscar Slater* and it was an overnight sensation. It produced an immediate clamour from the public for Oscar Slater's release, and in just over 18 months he was freed from prison by the Scottish Court of Criminal Appeal and given £6,000 in compensation.

But, if Oscar Slater was innocent, who had killed the frail old woman?

Helen Lambie, the servant admonished by Miss Gilchrist's niece, kept silent about the man she believed to be the killer. Some top criminologists believed that the man was a highly placed public person, a man with a reputation to protect. That was the theory shared by Conan Doyle, who said shortly before his death:

'I believe I know the identity of the real murderer, a man who was protected by the police because he was a prominent citizen who desperately wanted something from the private papers of Miss Marion Gilchrist. He has gone unpunished, but it is more important to me that an innocent man is free.'

What Miss Gilchrist's private papers contained has never been established and almost certainly never will be. It is believed they were deposited with a Scottish legal firm - where they probably sit to this day.

ARM IN THE SHARK

A bizarre and macabre plot, too farfetched for any crime novel, launched one of the world's most mysterious murder hunts. Not even Agatha Christie could have dreamed up the astonishing series of events that began with two crooks falling out, and ended with a murder trial at which no one was convicted.

The two crooks were minor Australian villains in Sydney's violent underworld of the 1930s. James Smith was a small-time thief and his partner John Brady a seedy conman. When they met in April 1935 to discuss the distribution of some loot, an argument developed. What occurred at that clandestine meeting remains a mystery, but it is assumed that Brady murdered Smith and hacked up his body. His remains were then placed in a metal trunk.

Every limb fitted inside but for the left arm, which Brady roped to the outside of the trunk. He then took his boat out into Gunnamatta Bay, off Sydney's eastern suburbs, and dumped the dreadful evidence of his crime into the sea.

A small shark would have been tempted by the smell of blood. It would have circled the trunk cautiously, coming ever closer until it felt brave enough to strike, severing the rope with its razor-sharp teeth. The arm would have floated free and the shark, we must assume, gulped it down whole.

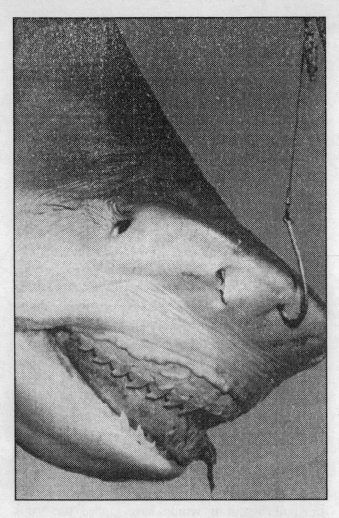

The Arm in the Shark case could never be solved, as the defence lawyer Mr Evatt pointed out, because an amputated limb did not prove that the owner was dead.

This grisly tale is, in part, surmise. But it is the only explanation for the extraordinary set of circumstances which now followed...

On 19 April 1935 a fisherman, Bert Hobson, was making an early morning examination of the lines he had baited with mackerel the day before. His quarry was shark – Tiger and White – which abounded off the Sydney coastline. About 450m/500yd offshore he saw that the water was being churned up by a shark in a feeding frenzy, the crazed state in which the beast, having smelled blood, thrashed around wildly, with its jaws snapping at anything that moved, caught Hobson's curiosity. As Hobson drew closer, he observed that a small shark, which had already become hooked on his line, was in the process of being devoured by a larger one. By the time Hobson had cautiously drawn his vessel alongside, the larger shark was also well and truly caught on his line.

Bert Hobson's unexpected catch – a superb specimen of a 3m/10ft Tiger shark – was so exhausted that there was no point in killing it. Hobson merely attached the length of line to his boat and turned for shore with his prize in tow. There was another reason why the fishermen did not wish to dispatch his prize catch. Hobson's brother Charles ran an aquarium at nearby Coogee Beach and needed a large shark to thrill and frighten his visitors.

And that was where Sharky, as he was now nicknamed, ended up. Charles Hobson's customers gawped at this killer of the deep through glass panels in his huge pool for seven days. Then on 25 April, Australia's Anzac Day, the visitors to Coogee Aquarium were met with a sickening sight.

Sharky went into convulsions, regurgitating all sorts of half-digested debris. Birds, rats and part of the smaller shark it had eaten were all disgorged. So was a human arm, attached to a piece of rope.

This was enough to send the day trippers running for home – and Charles Hobson straight to the police. He fished out the arm while he waited for them to arrive. On examination it appeared to be the left arm of a man; tattooed on it were two boxers.

Naturally enough, police at first believed that the arm had been torn from a swimmer by one of the myriad sharks that infested the Sydney shoreline. They explained the presence of the rope with the theory that the unfortunate victim may have been swimming for shore with a small boat in tow. But they were forced to change their minds when a police pathologist reported that the arm had been neatly severed with a sharp clasp knife, not ripped from the body by the jagged teeth of a shark. Besides which, no one had recently been reported missing in a swimming accident.

With great difficulty, because of the state of the limb, fingerprints were taken, and were found to match those of a man on police files: a club owner named James Smith, who already had a police record for illegal gambling.

Smith had been missing from his home for almost a month. When detectives called on his widow, Gladys, she was able to tell them only that, as far as she knew, her 33-year-old husband had gone on a fishing trip. And she was not concerned that he had not returned – long stays away from the marital home were a regular occurrence.

The police began interviewing the dead man's friends and accomplices, and eventually tracked down one John Brady – with difficulty because he was wanted by Tasmanian police for questioning over forgery allegations. They found him on 17 May living with his wife in a squalid rented flat in North Sydney. Brady admitted that he and Smith had stayed in a cottage at Gunnamatta Bay, where the shark was caught, but he adamantly denied knowing anything about a murder.

Nevertheless, police charged Brady with murder. They believed that the case was provable. They claimed that James Smith and John Brady had stayed together while planning their next fraud. The pair fell out, possibly over the distribution of the spoils, and Brady murdered his accomplice. Brady hacked up the body, stuffed it in a metal trunk, apart from the left arm which he roped to the outside. He then took his boat out into Gunnamatta Bay and dumped the dreadful evidence. They theorised that the dead man's arm was trailing in the water when it was swallowed by the smaller shark – eventually to be eaten by the large Tiger which ended up in Coogee Aquarium.

What was the crime that the two had been plotting? Through underworld informants, detectives reckoned it to be an insurance fraud on a yacht that had recently disappeared. The vessel's former owner was a key witness and they made an appointment to interview him. They were too late, however. On the very eve of the inquest into Smith's death, the yacht owner was found sitting silently in his car, parked under the approaches of the famous Sydney Harbour Bridge. He had been shot dead.

Nevertheless, the inquest went ahead. Among the grisly exhibits called for were two pieces of skin with tattoo marks on them. It was by these mortal remains of her husband that Gladys Smith had identified the dead man at the city morgue. At one stage in the inquest, the police prosecutor asked the government medical officer, Dr Aubrey Palmer: 'Have you the pieces of skin with you?'

He replied: 'I have them. But I do not usually produce dead bodies, or parts of dead bodies, unless the court ask me to do so.'

The court did indeed ask – and the two pieces of skin were tendered and marked for exhibit.

This was part of the dialogue between the police prosecutor, Sergeant William Toole, and Dr Palmer.

Sgt Toole: 'Would it be possible for a man to remove his arm himself in the manner in which you found it?'

Dr Palmer: 'I think it extremely unlikely that a

man could remove it himself. It is not a thing he could do with one sweep, although it is remarkable what terrible wounds some people, lunatics, do inflict on themselves.'

Sgt Toole: 'Have you had any experience in connection with the digestion of sharks?'

Dr Palmer: 'Yes. It is a cold-blooded animal and the digestion is slow, more especially in cold water. Sometimes they starve for some time and then when they have a feed it takes some time to digest, from days to weeks.'

Sgt Toole: 'If the arm had been swallowed by a small shark and the small shark swallowed by a large shark, would that have any effect on the arm?'

Dr Palmer:

'No doubt the digestion would be slower. There would be a certain amount of shark digested first, although there might be some digestive juices left in the swallowed shark. But I should think that there would not be much digestion by the swallowed shark, so the swallowed shark would have to be digested first. But in any case, there would not be anything unusual about an arm remaining in a shark for a week without being digested.'

Then Mr Clive Evatt, the barrister briefed for Brady, played his trump card. He asked Dr Palmer: 'I suppose you agree that it is conceivable that if as much of the human arm as existed in this case … were torn or cut off the trunk in a train accident or by machinery, that the individual could survive?'

Palmer replied: 'That is so, I agree.'

Evatt continued: 'There are two conclusions that I put to you – that there is no evidence available as to how the man died, that is, assuming he is dead, and secondly, the individual from whom the arm came could still be alive today?'

Palmer said: 'I would not deny the possibility, but I could hardly conceive that he would be.'

Mr Evatt stuck to his trump card in the trial that followed. In law, the discovery of an amputated limb did not prove its owner dead! The court agreed with him – and John Brady's trial for murder was halted by the judge after only two days with a direction to the jury to acquit him.

In a separate case, signed statements taken from the yacht owner before his murder were judged inadmissible as evidence in court, and the two men charged with killing him also went free.

What of John Brady? The petty crook continued his career of crime, spending another 20 years of his life behind bars. He died of a heart attack at the age of 71 in a prison repatriation hospital. And with him died hopes of uncovering the grisly secrets of the Arm in the Shark case.

THE A1 MURDER: JANICE WESTON

A lonely, rain-spattered lay-by on the A1 Great North Road is a place for emergency stops as traffic thunders by, a refuge for a tired truck driver to grab a few minutes sleep – and a place for the perfect murder.

In a few frenzied moments on a windswept Saturday night the most grisly of crimes was committed – and the most mysterious, because of the almost complete lack of clues.

Years on, no flowers mark the asphalt where solicitor Janice Weston died in a brutal assault in her car. No culprit has been brought to book because the seemingly motiveless crime was, and looks like it will remain, impossible to solve.

The crime intrigued both the veteran policemen called in to investigate it and the legions of Fleet Street journalists following in their footsteps. All searched in vain for facts, clues, suspects and all returned to their respective stations and offices as baffled as when they set out.

For journalists in particular it was, in the well-worn Fleet Street phrase, 'a damn good story'. It contained those magic ingredients of glamour, money, power, love and, of course, murder most foul. This is Janice Weston's story.

The brutal murder of the successful and beautiful solicitor Janice Weston in a lonely lay-by still confounds the unfortunate people involved.

It begins at Manchester, where Janice Weston shone in the city's university; she read law after leaving her convent school in Finchley, north London, with nine O-levels and four A-levels.

There, as at home and school and with her friends, she was distinguished not only by hard work and application but by a cheerful personality and charm, which endeared her to everyone she met.

She qualified in law and while still young, in professional terms, landed a plum job with the top London law firm of Herbert Oppenheimer, Nathan and Vandyck. It was there she was to meet two key men in her life – indeed, one could say the two most important men in her life.

One was Tony Weston, a property developer who, although already married, was to become her husband. The other was Heinz Isner, 41 years her senior and a powerful merchant banker who had fled persecution in Hitler's Germany shortly before the outbreak of the Second World War.

One man she was to fall in love with. The other, Isner, was to love her. He even once asked her to marry him, but she politely turned him down. In her capacity as legal adviser to his company, she remained a faithful friend and confidante, accompanying him to dinners, the theatre and trips to the ballet.

Her career continued to blossom. She became acknowledged as a leading expert on computer law just at the time when the use of new technology in commerce rocketed. She was immediately recognised for her talents and was snapped up by the top Lincoln's Inn practice Charles Russell and Company as a partner.

Janice was badly affected when Isner died in 1977. She had spoken of her fondness for the kind old gentleman, but she was staggered by the extent to which he cared for her. In his will he left her close to £142,000 worth of shares, cash, paintings, furniture and antiques from his vast estate.

Janice, then 30, was rapidly becoming financially secure in her own right, as her worth was rewarded in high salaries and perks. Her boss, Lord Nathan, was later to remark that she was one of the most brilliant corporate lawyers he had ever known, and had mastered the complexities of huge companies and the stock exchange almost single-handedly.

In 1982, after a long wait for his divorce to come through, she married Tony Weston. It was a quiet affair and for Janice was the peak of her short, successful life. She had money, success, status, wealth, a luxurious London home and the man she loved. Life was good indeed.

Tony Weston, too, was a success. A quiet man in business as well as social life, he beavered away on property deals and, together with Janice, invested in a run-down mansion called Clopton Manor in Northamptonshire, which they could modernise and turn into apartments. Janice put up some of her capital, and they both moved into part of the building as a weekend retreat.

On 10 September 1983 Janice was doing research on a new computer law book. Her husband was in France negotiating to buy a Louis XVII château in the Loire valley as part of his business. It was the last day of Janice Weston's short life.

Necessarily, because of what was to happen, fact and speculation mingle in the final hours that Janice had left to her. It is fact that a partner in the firm where she worked turned up at the law offices at about 5pm and saw her working there.

It is fact that detectives who were later to search her home in London's Holland Park found there the traces of a scant meal and the remnants of a bottle of wine, with the cutlery and crockery not washed up. There was one wine glass, indicating that she had dined alone. Also there was her handbag but, mysteriously, not her purse – two items, detectives were later to ponder, that were usually inseparable from Janice Weston.

It is fact that she got into her silver Alfa Romeo and drove off north to the place where her life was to end. But apart from this cameo scene of a London home, which looked as if it had been left in a hurry, police had little to guide them as they took the painful road from fact into theory.

Why had she left in a hurry? Why had this normally most fastidious of women left the washing up undone? Why was there no message in her flat signifying a hasty exit or a clue from her husband in France as to why she was gone? And why was she beaten to death in that narrow, insignificant lay-by on the northbound section of the A1, just 22.5km/14miles from Clopton Manor?

For that is what happened to Janice, either late that Saturday night or in the very early hours of Sunday. It was 9am on Sunday 11 September that a racing cyclist stopped in the lay-by, looked in the ditch and saw Janice Weston's body. Of her car, there was no sign.

Pedalling probably faster than he had ever done in his life, the cyclist reached a hotel further down the road and alerted police. That was the signal for the head of Cambridgeshire Criminal Ivestigation Department, Detective Chief Superintendent Len Bradley, to become involved in the most baffling murder case of his career. When he arrived at the scene, even he was shocked at the brutality of the crime, at the force with which Janice had been attacked.

Bradley, a blunt Yorkshireman, totally dedicated and highly respected, embarked on a murder enquiry that was to cost thousands of man hours, hundreds of thousands of pounds and untold mental stress on himself and his detectives. It spanned the length and breadth of Britain and even stretched to the continent. But it was, ultimately, in the face of baffling circumstances and lack of clues, to fail.

As the rain pelted into his face on that Sunday morning, Detective Chief Superintendent Bradley quickly confirmed the cause of death, identifying the jack found near her body as the murder weapon. The pathologist said that she probably died between 9pm on Saturday and 2am on Sunday.

The question police faced was how a woman dressed in jeans and jumper, with no identification on her, came to be beaten to death in a lay-by on the A1. And, since her car was missing, poor Janice Weston remained unidentified for 48 hours.

It wasn't until colleagues at her law firm became worried about her absence that they notified Janice's sister, who in turn contacted police. Only then were they able to give the body the dignity of an identity. Twenty-four hours later, an eagle-eyed policeman in the Camden area of London spotted the abandoned – and bloodstained – Alfa Romeo.

Tony Weston hurried back from France and issued an appeal for anyone with information to come forward. One lead gave the police some hope...

A man phoned them from a car repairs shop in Royston, Hertfordshire, 48km/30 miles from the scene of the murder, and said that at 11am on the morning her body was found, when the press had not yet broken the story of her death, a man aged between 25 and 30 had walked into his shop and ordered two spare car plates with the same registration number as her car. The man, seen by witnesses, has never been traced. It is as if he vanished into thin air.

Then, the police concentrated on the Alfa's missing spare tyre. Janice Weston did, it was confirmed later, go to a garage first thing on Saturday morning, her last day alive, to collect a repaired tyre which had her husband's name and telephone number chalked on it. The garage mechanic put it in the boot, leaving the old spare on the vehicle. But when the Alfa was found, the repaired tyre was back on the car and the spare was missing. Why?

Lawmen went through all the usual possibilities and motives. They ranged from the possible – that Janice had made a rendezvous with a secret lover who lured her to her death – to the overdramatic – that she had been silenced because her law research had stumbled on some ultra-sensitive secret.

All enquiries drew a blank. Janice Weston did not dabble in affairs of the heart. It was unlikely she was heading towards her Northamptonshire home, because the rooms there were not made up. And the peripheral possibilities, such as the suggestion that she gave a lift to a deranged hitchhiker are not given much credence by police.

To cover all avenues, detective were despatched to France to check on Tony Weston's movements on the weekend that his wife met her death. He was held, in December of that year, for 55 hours and a report was prepared by the Cambridgeshire police, but no charges were ever levelled against him.

So it was not the husband. It was not a lover. It was not a mad hitchhiker or some sinister dubious agent of hi-tech espionage. The secret of who killed Janice Weston was lost in the wind and the rain of that dark, terrible night.

LIZZIE BORDEN

Lizzie Borden took an axe
And gave her mother forty whacks.
When she saw what she had done
She gave her father forty-one!

The rhyme haunted her until the day Lizzie Borden died. It was sung innocently by children in the school playground; it was chanted tauntingly in the street as she passed by. And yet Lizzie was, as a jury had clearly decided, wholly innocent of the bloody crime.

Or was she?

The saga of Lizzie Borden began in 1860 when she was born to a loving mother and a rich, but miserly father in the Massachusetts textile town of Fall River. Her full name was Lizzie Andrew – because her father had wanted a boy. Andrew J Borden was extremely wealthy yet the household at 92 Second Street was not a happy one. The house was filthy, the conditions insanitary. The old man hoarded his money and did not believe in enjoying its benefits on earth.

A mean-spirited puritan who was reckoned to be the meanest man in Fall River, Andrew Borden had, first as an undertaker, then as a property speculator, amassed a personal fortune in excess of half a million dollars. He never lavished it on his wife Sarah, and he

The tragic saga of Lizzie Borden didn't end when she was acquitted of the murder of her father and stepmother. She still had to listen to the children's taunts: 'Lizzie Borden took an axe...'

certainly did not do so on his two daughters, Lizzie and her elder sister Emma.

Sarah Borden died when Lizzie was just two years of age. Her father waited only a further two years before remarrying. The new union, between Andrew Borden and Abby Gray, was hardly a marriage made in heaven. From the start, there seemed to be little love between the two. Abby, a plump 37-year-old, was treated more as a housekeeper than a bride by her 41-year-old husband. Neither was she much better treated by her stepchildren, both of whom thought she was a golddigger after their father's money.

Lizzie Borden was infuriated when she discovered that her father was indeed planning to spend some of his hard-earned money – not on his children, but on the sister of the stepmother she detested. Her father, in an uncharacteristic display of generosity, had saved the step-aunt from financial ruin by giving her a sum of money. Lizzie was furious and plotted revenge.

When her father and stepmother were out of the house, she ransacked their bedroom, pocketed some cheap jewellery and blamed it on burglars. It took little detective work to prove that the only sneak-thief who had been at work that day was the jealous Lizzie Borden. The atmosphere in the unhappy household deteriorated further. But now outsiders also knew of the simmering hatred which Lizzie Borden harboured for her stepmother.

In the summer of 1892, Fall River sweltered in a heat wave and tempers frayed. When thieves twice broke into the garden sheds at Number 92, old man Borden took bizarre steps to prevent a repeat of the crime. Convinced that the intruders were after Lizzie's pet pigeons, he took an axe and decapitated every one of the birds.

By August the heat had become so oppressive that many of the townsfolk had left Fall River to stay with relatives in cooler regions. Emma decided to move in with friends at the country town of Fairhaven, 32 km/20 miles away. Lizzie, now aged 32, decided to remain at home.

A curious series of food poisonings occurred that month. Both Mr and Mrs Borden and their servant, Bridget Sullivan, were twice afflicted with severe stomach cramps. Lizzie, however, seemed unaffected.

On 4 August, the hottest day of the year, Lizzie arose from her bed late, claiming that she too had now been affected by the food bug. At 9am she wandered into the kitchen. The only person who saw her was Bridget, who was ironing some clothes.

At 9.30am Mrs Borden was crouched over, cleaning some steps leading to the spare bedroom of the house. Without warning, she was struck from behind by a single, sharp blow with an axe. It was enough to kill her instantly, but it was followed by eight more in quick succession. The room was awash with blood.

Just before 11am, Mr Borden returned home after a morning checking on his businesses throughout the town. He was flustered from the heat and obviously in some discomfort, having been walking far too briskly. Lizzie fussed around him, telling him to sit down out of the heat. Told by Lizzie that her stepmother had gone out, the old man settled down for a snooze on the settee. Lizzie meanwhile wandered into the kitchen to gossip with Bridget who, like Lizzie, had suffered from the same mild bout of food poisoning, brought on by a joint of mutton which had been cooked for them by Mrs Borden some days previously and had not been stored properly.

Bridget Sullivan was later to tell detectives that she heard the house clock strike eleven as she climbed the stairs to her own bed to nurse her upset stomach. However, she was flying down the stairs again ten minutes later as the screaming, demented Lizzie bawled: 'Come down, come down. Father's dead. Someone came in and killed him!'

But when Bridget reached the living room, Lizzie would not let her in. Instead she ordered her out to fetch the local doctor, a man called Bowen. He wasn't available, so Lizzie despatched the frantic maid to go and find one of her friends. When Bowen eventually turned up, he found that Andrew Borden had been mutilated by blow after blow from an axe. The doctor could only lay a sheet over the corpse as neighbour Adelaide Churchill tried to comfort Lizzie Borden.

Lizzie, however, seemed perfectly calm (a fact not overlooked when the police arrived later). A search of the house by Mrs Churchill and Alice Russell, another friend of Lizzie, revealed the body of her stepmother lying where she had been struck down on the steps leading to the spare bedroom.

Lizzie Borden's behaviour grew ever more curious. When Bridget Sullivan asked where she had been when her father was killed, Lizzie said she was out in the yard. When Mrs Churchill asked her the same question, she said she had been in the barn to get a piece of iron. She told that story to the police, adding that she had eaten three pears while searching the barn – but a police search revealed dust and debris and no sign of pear cores.

Police suspicion at first centred on John Morse, the brother of Mr Borden's first wife, who had stayed with the family for a few days before moving on to visit other relatives. However, he had an alibi and, although he had returned to the house close to the time of the killings, detectives were satisfied with his explanation of his whereabouts.

All suspicion now seemed to centre on Lizzie Borden. A check had been made with the pharmacy in town, which confirmed that the day before the murders she had bought some deadly prussic acid. She said she had not seen the body of her stepmother as she came down the stairs to see her father. She had told Mrs Russell the previous evening that her father had enemies and she was frightened that a revenge attack would occur soon. The police were sure that the murders had been carried out by someone in the household – and, after Morse had been ruled out, that left just Lizzie Borden and Bridget Sullivan.

Bridget Sullivan was dismissed as a suspect because there was no motive for her to kill; she stood to gain nothing from legacies and there was no money in the house. Besides, in the world of that emotionally strained household, Bridget was the one person liked by everyone.

No, it all came back to Lizzie Borden. Everyone knew that she hated the second Mrs Borden, they had heard about the fake burglary and, now, her strange behaviour. The offhand, arrogant way she dealt with the police questioning – as if she was deigning to speak to them 'like she were a grand lady holding court', as one officer described her attitude – did nothing but confirm police suspicions.

Secretly an arrest warrant was drawn up to hold Lizzie Borden, but it was not served. The police wanted to hear her evidence at the inquest; if they charged her too soon, it was possible that she could plead a right to silence at her trial and the mystery might never be solved.

A recently cleaned axe head was found in the cellar of the Borden house and was confiscated by detectives. Also, unbeknown to Lizzie Borden, the heads of the bodies were removed before their burial for specialist forensic examination. This revealed, in the words of the official report: '…injuries consistent with a frenzied, almost psychopathic attack, although both victims died with the first blow such was the force with which it was delivered.'

The inquest began early in September and was held

in secret. From the start, Lizzie incriminated herself, issuing contradictory statements which only further aroused suspicions of the investigating authorities. She said at the hearing that she had not been on the stairs when her father arrived home; rather, that she was in the kitchen. 'I thought I was on the stairs but now I know I was in the kitchen,' she said.

When asked as to why she had changed her story, she said confidently, without hesitation: 'Looking back on this dreadful event has made me recall things much more clearly.'

Long before Lizzie Borden stood in the witness box at the inquest, she had been judged and sentenced by the fourth estate – the newspapers. The press, fuelled by the wild rumours which flourished after the murders, came down firmly on the side of public opinion that this quiet, God-fearing woman, who belonged to the Women's Christian Temperance Union was indeed the same person who had killed Mr and Mrs Borden.

The public prosecutor in Massachusetts confided to the attorney general that he was not confident of a conviction if the case went to trial, but that there was no other suspect. It would all hinge on how the trial was conducted.

Lizzie Borden came to trial in June 1893. By then fickle public opinion had turned full circle. The folk of Massachusetts, infuriated by the barrage of smears against their God-fearing citizen, began to believe that Lizzie was innocent after all.

Lizzie Borden was also fortunate in her choice of advocate. She appointed one of the best criminal lawyers in the state, George Robinson, a former governor of Massachusetts, who, while in that office, had been responsible for appointing one of the three judges who now sat on the bench before him. The judge repaid the favour by agreeing with Robinson that damning transcripts of Lizzie's questioning at the inquest were inadmissible. The court also disallowed statements about the purchase by Lizzie of prussic acid the day before the murders.

As the trial went on, the prosecution case looked weaker and weaker. Much of it depended on what was not even circumstantial evidence. All it boiled down to in the end was the fact that Lizzie Borden was in the house at the time of the murders and that her evidence was conflicting.

The hostility she felt for her stepmother was played down by Mrs Russell and Bridget Sullivan, who said that it had been blown out of proportion. And there was an emotional coup for the defence when Lizzie fainted in the dock midway through the 10-day hearing, an act which secured her immense sympathy from the jury, who were fast being led to believe that the state was the villain of the piece for ever allowing this poor creature to be put on trial.

Robinson played on the emotions of the jury, at one stage pointing to the refined and neatly dressed Lizzie and asking: 'To find her guilty, you must believe she is a fiend. Gentlemen, does she look it?'

For the prosecution, one of the theories advanced was that Lizzie suffered a special kind of epilepsy, usually brought on by her menstrual cycle. While she was in the grip of one of these attacks, it was suggested, she murdered her parents and was left with no memory of the crime. It was thin stuff, however, without the benefit of forensic clues or witnesses.

Amid a cacophony of public cheers, Lizzie stepped from the dock a free – and rich – woman. She inherited much of her father's wealth and, instead of moving away from Fall River, she bought a property in a wealthy suburb, and forever after braved the echoes of the taunts that followed the slaughter at Number 92.

The Borden case was never reopened by the police. They seemed convinced that justice had been cheated and that the real killer had walked from the dock a free woman. Certainly there were never any more axe slayings in the little Massachusetts community.

Rumours spread that the killings were an elaborate plot hatched between Lizzie Borden and the maid, Bridget Sullivan. Bridget soon returned to Ireland, where she had been born, replete, it was said, with cash from the late Mr Borden's bank account, which had been generously donated to her by Lizzie.

Lizzie Borden initially lived with her sister Emma, but they argued and eventually the friendless spinster resided alone, almost a recluse, until she died at the age of 67 in 1927. She was buried in the same family plot as the victims who had died on that sweltering

August day 35 years before.

Was she guilty? Certainly if you believe the film in which Elizabeth Montgomery portrayed Lizzie Borden as murderess – hacking her stepmother and father to death while naked, in order to avoid blood splashes on her dress. A further five stage plays about her were written, as well as countless books and essays on the case. Still the mystery remains.

One person who believes she committed the murders during an attack of epilepsy is Victoria Lincoln who says in her book *A Private Disgrace*: 'During a seizure there are periods of automatic action which in some cases the patient forgets completely and in others remembers only dimly.'

The woman whose reputation is tainted with this most awful of crimes still arouses fierce passions. There is a Friends of Lizzie Borden Society in America to this day, which continues to revere her cleared name. Others still prefer to believe that it was she who struck her father and stepmother with an axe. Whatever either side believes, it is a secret which now can never be proved.

GLENN MILLER

On a December afternoon in 1944 two American officers boarded a plane at Twinwoods airfield, north of London, and, accompanied only by their pilot, took off on a routine flight across the English Channel to France. None of the men were ever seen again. The disappearance would perhaps be considered only a minor tragedy in the bloody history of the Second World War, but the story still intrigues the world decades later because of the identity of one of the officers.

Lost on that mysterious journey was the band leader Glenn Miller, one of the best loved musicians of the century. Did he die in the icy waters of the Channel? Did he engineer his own disappearance? Or, as has been suggested, was he murdered?

Glenn Miller's hits, such as 'String of Pearls', 'Moonlight Serenade' and 'In the Mood', had been part of the war effort. His celebrated big-band sound had been heard from New York to North Africa, from Sydney to Sicily, bringing to a world ravaged by war a musical style that was both harmonious and happy. Recognising this feel good factor, the Allied supreme commander, General Dwight D Eisenhower, encouraged Miller to broadcast from London to boost morale in the build up to the invasion of France. After the successful invasion, Miller himself decided to take his 60-piece orchestra onto the Continent and follow the war across Europe, inspiring the soldiers along the way.

That was why, on 15 December 1944, Glenn Miller travelled to the remote airfield in Twinwoods, Bedfordshire, and boarded the plane bound for Paris to sort out arrangements for one of the biggest and most eagerly awaited concerts of all time.

Miller, aged 40 at the time, was travelling to the recently liberated French capital to prepare a Christmas concert for the British and American servicemen occupying the city. Normally his manager would have made the arrangements but Miller, for some unexplained reason, decided to make the trip himself. The band, composed of air force personnel, was to follow on a later flight.

The aircraft Miller and his fellow officer were provided with was a single-engine Norseman D-64, renowned throughout the service for its reliability and sturdiness. There were fog warnings – sufficient to ground all Royal Air Force training flights that day – but the pilot was completely confident that he could handle the weather conditions. Yet nothing of the pilot, Miller and his colleague, or the aircraft, has ever been seen again. No wreckage was found, no bodies, nothing.

Two days after Miller's disappearance, his band, having arrived in Paris on schedule, were still waiting for him, puzzled that he had not turned up to greet them. No explanation was ever given to them and they could only guess at their leader's demise. When the millions of his fans learned of his disappearance, the tragedy was compounded by the fact that there was no grave to his memory, no monument to turn into a shrine. To this day, exactly how Glenn Miller met his tragic end remains a complete mystery.

The theory most widely accepted at the time was that ice had formed on the aircraft, the extra weight dragging it down towards the waters of the English Channel, and all its occupants were presumed drowned. Over the years, however, a whole host of strange, not to say disquieting, theories have arisen.

Many of Miller's fans failed to accept the War Ministry's simple crash theory, believing that there had been a cover-up. Perhaps his plane had been shot down in error by a British fighter. More romantically, was he a spy engaged in a secret mission that ended disastrously in France? Or had he been so badly disfigured by the crash that he preferred to spend the rest of his life in solitude? Did he suffer amnesia?

And yet why should Glenn Miller have decided to engineer his own disappearance? He was, perhaps, the most popular musician in the world. His unique sound could be heard in every dance hall in the Western world. He had a portfolio of unpublished scores in his case aboard the Paris-bound plane. Music had made Miller and his band rich and the people who listened to it happy. And Miller knew that when the Second World War ended, he could step out of the uniform of a US Army captain and resume his life as a professional musician.

One man, John Edwards, became obsessed by the disappearance of the band leader and spent a small fortune in researching how he met his end. Edwards, a former RAF pilot, devoted two decades to trying to solve the riddle in an investigation that cost him about £10,000. His theory is now one of the most contentious: that Miller, a well-known womaniser, was not killed as the result of a flying accident, but that he was murdered.

Edwards claims to have interviewed a witness who says he saw Miller switch planes shortly after the Norseman had taken off. The plane, it is claimed, went only as far as a nearby airfield at Bovingdon, Hertfordshire – where Miller switched to a Dakota transport, which then flew him on to France. The reason for such an elaborate flight plan is unknown.

Edwards says that Miller did make it to Paris – only to meet an untimely and ignominious death three days later. According to Edwards, the sex-mad musician died of a fractured skull in the Pigalle district, the notorious haunt of pimps and prostitutes. His death was then covered-up by American military leaders anxious to avoid a morale-damaging scandal surrounding such a national hero.

A bizarre story, certainly, but as Edwards says:

'Why was there no official full inquiry? I have met great difficulty in trying to solve this mystery. Records have been reported burned. Other information, like the aircrew report, is unaccountably vague. Even the weather conditions were listed as unknown. But pieces of information I collected over the years eventually all fell into place. I have evidence that an American military doctor in Paris signed Miller's death certificate. A retired US Air Force lieutenant colonel recalls being told by the Provost Marshall's police office in Paris that Miller had been murdered. And I know a man in Miller's band who stated that it was common knowledge to those close to him that his boss was murdered in Paris.'

Edwards is not the only one who believes that there was something suspicious about the last flight of the band leader. In 1978 a medium called Carmen Rogers held an eerie psychic session at the deserted Twinwoods airfield. She said:

'I could see Glenn Miller walking to the aircraft with two other men. Miller was disturbed and worried about his domestic and other affairs. He did not want to make the trip to Paris. He felt sick and afraid. After they took off, Miller asked the pilot to land. The pilot put down as soon as possible and let Miller get out. The aircraft touched down on the Essex side of the Thames estuary. Then Miller got out and made a phone call to London and arranged his own disappearance.'

Many theories have been put forward – whether it be that he was a spy on a mission or that he contracted amnesia – and many wrecked aircraft have been found in the Channel. But never the skeleton of Glenn Miller's Norseman D-64.

DIANE JONES

It had all the hallmarks of a Ruth Rendell mystery. The setting was a quaint, old English beauty spot; there was the sober-suited village doctor, his attractive wife, a mysterious disappearance, a great deal of scandal bubbling just beneath the surface – and a violent murder.

The difference between a murder thriller and this particular case is that in fiction the crime is always solved and the police usually apprehend the culprit. When the wife of the village doctor went missing, however, the crime was never solved, the case was never closed and the mystery remains to this day.

The real-life saga of English rural life began on the night of 23 July 1983 in the village of Coggeshall in the Essex countryside. It was a night when Diane Jones, aged 35, again had too much to drink in the local pub, The Woolpack.

Diane was the third wife of Doctor Robert Jones, who was five years her senior. She had been a patient of the doctor, and they had first met when he was treating her for depression. They were married in 1982 but the marriage was not happy – stormy was the word most used by locals to describe it. Diane was known in the village as a rather eccentric woman who drank too much. The Woolpack was one of the few places where she was seen regularly in the company of her husband.

Dr Robert Jones was the first person police suspected when his wife Diane mysteriously disappeared, as their marriage was known to be quite turbulent.

The first hint that all was not well with the relationship was when Dr Jones arrived to his surgery one morning with two black eyes. He had been in a fight with one of Diane's ex-lovers, swimming pool attendant Paul Barnes. Soon afterwards Diane was arrested for dangerous driving and theft of a bottle of champagne from a hotel and, after the court case, made some astonishing allegations to reporters. She announced that her husband repeatedly threw her out of the house and that he had punched her.

Dr Jones replied to this accusation: 'Diane used to go on these benders and smash the place up. I had to use violence to restrain her.' Their marriage was clearly turbulent, and their baby daughter was taken into care because the social services considered that the marital home was not safe for the child.

On the last night before Diane Jones disappeared, both she and her husband were in The Woolpack. She was drinking heavily and the pub echoed to her raucous laughter. Dr Jones ordered her to quieten down and a blazing row ensued. The evening ended when she toppled from her bar stool and he carried her out of the pub. She was never seen alive again.

There was no sign of Diane in the village the next day. Dr Jones opened his surgery as usual, where patients were greeted by his receptionist Sue Smith, his ex-wife who had since remarried. As the days passed, locals noticed that Mrs Jones had not been seen around the village. The doctor explained that he had taken her home after her binge in the Woolpack, but that she had later run off into the night.

Nine days passed before Dr Jones reported that his wife had vanished. 'She has often disappeared before,' he told police. They were not convinced – and neither were the press, who swooped on Coggeshall en masse. They interviewed a number of Mrs Jones's ex-lovers about their nights of passion with the doctor's wife. Headlines cataloguing her wild abandon greeted the doctor each morning. Even his ex-wife Sue, now married to wealthy antiques dealer John Smith, revealed to a newspaper that it was the doctor's infidelity that had led her to divorce him on grounds of adultery.

Dr Jones himself admitted that his marriage to Diane had reached breaking point. He said that he was exasperated by her drinking and by her string of lovers. But he stressed that he had not harmed his wife on the night she vanished.

Nevertheless, the police searched his home. The doctor suffered the ignominy of having his garden dug up, his floorboards pulled up, his furniture removed and he endured hours of questioning by detectives. They discovered nothing. The doctor put on a brave face at the suspicion and innuendo levelled at him. He attended his surgery regularly and tried, amidst the publicity, to lead a normal life. But he was never out of the headlines. He was charged with drunk driving just weeks after Diane had vanished, the result of a night he had spent drinking with his old adversary, Paul Barnes.

Throughout the summer and into the autumn Dr Jones endured the attention of the world's press. Then on 23 October, three months to the day since her disappearance, beaters on a pheasant shoot found her corpse 48km/30 miles from Coggeshall, in a wood at Brightwell, Suffolk. A pathologist who examined her badly decomposed body discovered that she had been three months pregnant.

In a dawn swoop at three homes on 14 November, Dr Jones, his ex-wife Sue Smith and Paul Barnes were taken in for questioning. After 12 hours Mrs Smith emerged to say: 'I don't know why they took me in for questioning but it was all very amicable.' Dr Jones, however, was questioned for three days.

While he was in custody, experts from the Home Office forensic laboratory in Huntingdon, Cambridgeshire, arrived at his home. They cordoned off the two-acre garden, excavated much of it and searched the area with metal detectors. Even the metal gate across the entrance to the driveway was dismantled and taken away to police headquarters for further forensic examination.

Then, as abruptly as he was arrested, Dr Jones was freed. He was told to report back to the police in 1984 when their enquiries had continued further. He did so only to be told finally that he had been officially ruled out of the investigation into his wife's mysterious death. The hunt for the killer was discontinued, the pressmen faded away and the village of Coggeshall returned to normal.

But the case of Diane Jones, one of the greatest unsolved murder mysteries, which has left the police completely baffled and fired the imaginations of crime writers, remains open.

THE KENNEDY ASSASSINATION

Most thought it was a firework or a police motorcycle backfiring. It certainly didn't sound like a gunshot; it was more of a sharp crack. Dallas dress manufacturer Abraham Zapruder was filming the presidential motorcade with his cine camera at the time and, although he heard the sound, he did not take his eye off the viewfinder. A road sign obscured his vision for a moment and when the Lincoln emerged from behind it, at a sedate 11 miles per hour, Zapruder saw John F Kennedy reaching for his throat. The dumbfounded cameraman thought the president was play-acting. He continued filming.

Though a bullet had passed through Kennedy's neck, the wound was not fatal. But, in the confusion of the moment, his Secret Service driver did not immediately react and for several seconds the powerful Lincoln actually slowed down. More shots rang out.

As Jackie Kennedy turned to her husband, Texas Governor John B Connally slumped forward with a bullet wound in his chest. Behind, agent Clint Hill quickly jumped from the following secret service car's running board and sprinted desperately towards the presidential Lincoln.

Then Zapruder saw through his viewfinder what

JFK set off across the airport tarmac in Dallas, not knowing the tragic fate he was about to meet.

agent Hill saw close-up – a final bullet striking home with devastating effect and, in an explosion of red, tearing the president's skull apart...

Suddenly it was all over.

Only minutes or hours – or a lifetime – before, the handsome, dashing, charismatic president had flown into Texas with his beautiful wife Jackie at his side. He had rightly been anxious about his reception in the Lone Star state. Friends had warned him his campaign trip there might turn rough. Right-wing Texas was not a place where a liberal president could rely on a warm welcome.

Kennedy wanted to make the best possible entrance into Dallas, where he was to hold a political rally. So, after stepping off US Air Force One at Love Fields airport, he ordered the bullet-proof perspex roof of his limousine to be removed, so that the crowds might more easily see him. His secret service team were horrified; Dallas has one of the highest murder rates in the world and they had already been notified of a number of death threats.

Fears subsided, however, as the presidential motorcade entered the city. It was a hot day and the crowds were out in force. 'Thank you, thank you,' he responded to their clapping and cheering. John F Kennedy suddenly had good reason to feel buoyant that sunny Friday in Dallas.

By 12.29pm the open presidential Lincoln was on the city outskirts, five minutes from a waiting civic lunch. The secret service agents in the following car felt easier. The crowds were thinner here, and the danger of sniper fire from the city's high office blocks were receding.

Ahead loomed a squat, rust-coloured warehouse; the last tall building on the route: the Texas School Book Depository. Governor Connally, seated in front of the president, waved to a group of spectators. His wife Nellie turned to Kennedy and said: 'Mr President, you can't say Dallas doesn't love you.'

'That is very obvious,' smiled Kennedy. They were his last words.

Seconds later, John Fitzgerald Kennedy, president of the United States of America, at just 46 years of age the most powerful man in the world, was murdered in Dealey Plaza, in the heart of Dallas, Texas.

Decades later, the death of J F K remains not only one of the most heinous murders of the century, but also one of the most infuriatingly unsolved crimes of all time. Today those six seconds of violence in Dallas remain as intriguing, as murky and as utterly baffling as ever. Was Kennedy assassinated by a lone gunman? Or was he the victim of a conspiracy? Was it a Cuban plot? Did the communists have a hand in it? Or was a death contract put out by ultra-right-wing Texans?

According to the official Warren Commission report on the assassination the following year, a 24-year-old book depository employee, Lee Harvey Oswald, operating without accomplices, fired the shots that killed Kennedy. But was Oswald really a lone assassin? Or just a small cog in a carefully planned conspiracy?

Vice President Lyndon B Johnson, who had travelled in the motorcade and was sworn in as president the same afternoon, said in interviews years later that he had always believed more than one person was involved and strongly suspected a communist plot. Because Oswald was a professed Marxist, who had once defected to the USSR, Johnson saw in the killing the hand of either Soviet leader Nikita Khrushchev or Cuba's Fidel Castro.

Yet Johnson did not voice these fears at the time. He feared that proof of a communist conspiracy would start a backlash that 'could conceivably lead the country into war'. He almost certainly helped pressurise the Warren Commission into reaching its convenient 'lone nut' verdict. This also suited the FBI and CIA. Both intelligence agencies had Oswald on their files because of his past activities, and they would surely have faced charges of gross incompetence if it were shown they had failed to detect a major conspiracy involving a left-winger already known to them.

But while the lone nut thesis served many interests, it always rang hollow...

According to the commission, Lee Harvey Oswald killed Kennedy with an unknown number of shots fired from the window of a sixth-floor storage area at the Texas Book Depository. Certainly, it was by this window that three spent cartridge cases and a sniper's nest of cardboard boxes were found after the shooting. A rifle lay near by.

But it is impossible to ignore the unusual activities that occurred at ground level before, during and after the assassination. For it was there, on the so-called grassy knoll, roughly 91m/100yd from the book depository's sixth-floor window, that many investigators believe a second gunman lay in wait.

It was from the grassy mound that Abraham Zapruder, shouting out in horror, shot his historic film of the assassination. Immediately behind the amateur cameraman was a wooden fence, which marked the perimeter of Dealey Plaza. It would have made an ideal spot for a second assassin.

Zapruder himself described a shot coming from right behind him, which was louder than all the others and reverberated all around him. Of the dozen or so other people on the grassy knoll, almost all told a similar story. Four workers from the *Dallas Morning News* spoke of 'a horrible, ear-shattering noise coming from behind us'. Many more people, including secret servicemen, policemen and numerous spectators in or outside the book depository also placed the grassy knoll as a source of shooting. Of the many policemen who ran to the area, two reported the smell of gunpowder lingering in the bushes beside the perimeter fence.

Just before the shooting, several people had gone behind the fence in search of a good vantage spot. There a man had produced a badge, said he was a secret service agent and warned them to move away.

Yet at no time, before or after the shooting, were there any secret servicemen in Dealey Plaza, other than those in the motorcade.

Later, one of the spectators who had encountered the mystery man described how a shot had come from behind him as the motorcade passed by moments later – so close that he heard it 'whiz only inches over my left shoulder'. Other witnesses spoke of two men running away from the assassination scene onto railway tracks behind the fence. An off-duty policeman saw one man 'slipping and sliding' down the railway embankment into a car park, throw something into the back of a car and speed off. A railway worker, whose signal box overlooked the car park, described how he saw two strangers by the fence just before the shooting. When the shots were fired he saw 'a flash of light or smoke or something' in the bushes.

So how many gunmen were operating in Dealey Plaza? Governor Connally always rejected the official theory that the bullet which travelled through his chest and wrist and ended up almost undamaged in his thigh was the same one that had passed through Kennedy's neck. He always maintained he was struck about a second later, and Zapruder's film appears to bear this out. If Connally is right, there must have been more than one gunman firing from the rear, since the rifle found in the depository could not have fired two bullets in so short a time.

One firm suspect questioned around this time,

following a tip-off that he had been involved in the assassination, was an ex-airline pilot from New Orleans, David Ferrie. An extreme right-winger who hated Kennedy, Ferrie had for many years been an aide of the rich, ruthless crime boss Carlos Marcello.

David Ferrie had an alibi for the moment of the killing, but investigators have produced a mass of evidence to show he knew Oswald. The weekend of the assassination, Ferrie drove hundreds of miles through Texas, apparently in the panic-stricken belief that his library card might be found among Oswald's possessions. In 1966 he was requestioned in New Orleans following evidence that he had acquired large sums of money just before the assassination. Early in 1967 he was reportedly about to be arrested on suspicion that he had flown one or more assassins out of Dallas in a private aircraft. Just before the arrest, however, he was found dead – officially from natural causes, though he left two typed notes suggesting it had been suicide.

Only hours after Ferrie's death the body of his associate Eladio del Valle, also being sought for questioning about the assassination, was found in a car in Miami. Del Valle's skull was split open and he had been shot in the heart. He also had links with crime boss Marcello.

Despite the seeming involvement of other, more powerful conspirators in Kennedy's killing, there can be no reasonable doubt that Lee Harvey Oswald was heavily implicated. The rifle found in the depository

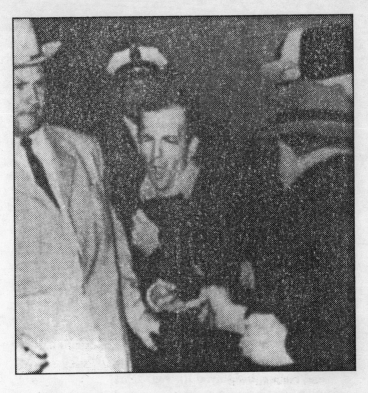

The killing of Lee Harvey Oswald by Jack Ruby, operator of a sleezy Dallas strip joint, initiated further questioning about the conspiracy theory.

was his, and he had brought a long package to work that morning supposedly containing curtain rods.

Back in Dallas on 22 November, Oswald was being interrogated. Despite the toughness of the questioning – and the millions of words that have been written about him since – Oswald remains the most enigmatic figure in the whole story of the Kennedy assassination.

A mass of contradictions, he was cunning, purposeful, of above average intelligence, yet strangely naive. At 16 he was apparently fascinated by communism, yet was determined to join one of the great symbols of American patriotism, the US Marines. Despite making no secret of his left-wing stance, he was posted to a top-secret US air base in Japan, which housed U-2 spy planes. Despite his access to military secrets, no one appears to have objected when he applied to travel to Russia, where he immediately renounced his United States citizenship and stayed for two years.

There is a plausible case to be made for his defection having been an elaborate charade organised by US military intelligence. Certainly, Oswald had no trouble getting back to the States, complete with Russian wife, when he became 'fed up' with the USSR two years later.

In 1963 he moved to New Orleans (Carlos Marcello's centre of operations) and became actively involved in left-wing politics, espousing the cause of Cuba's new communist dictator, Fidel Castro. Yet, at the same time, he was also apparently mixing with men of the extreme right.

In October that same year he moved to Dallas – by which time Kennedy's visit there had already been announced – and landed a job at the book depository. Then, on 22 November, the man who had never been heard to express anything but admiration for President John Fitzgerald Kennedy became the chief suspect in his killing.

After the assassination, things quickly went wrong for Oswald.

One of the first policemen to dash into the depository moments after the shooting found him calmly sipping Coca-Cola in the second-floor lunchroom. Within minutes, however, he had fled the scene. He went by bus and taxi to his lodgings, changed clothes, then set off up the road on foot.

Some 15 minutes later, about a mile from Oswald's lodgings, came yet another killing. Police patrolman JD Tippit stopped his car to speak to a man on the pavement. The man pulled out a pistol, gunned him down and ran off.

The Warren Commission ruled that Oswald, presumably fearing he was to be picked up for Kennedy's murder, was Tippit's killer.

Possibly a panic-stricken Oswald did indeed shoot Tippit, but it remains a puzzling incident. At the time, police had circulated only the briefest of descriptions of the sniper seen at window: 'White male, approximately 30, 165 pounds, slender build.' It could have fitted tens of thousands of Dallas inhabitants. Why did Tippit want to speak to this particular man?

Shortly after Tippit's death a shopkeeper saw Oswald go into a cinema, thought he looked suspicious and called the police who arrested him after a struggle. By the late afternoon of the assassination, everything was pointing to Oswald's guilt – perhaps just as had been planned.

In custody, Oswald repeatedly denied he had shot either Kennedy or Tippit and claimed several times he had been set up. 'I'm just a patsy,' he kept saying.

But a patsy for whom? If Oswald were about to justify his claim, he would need to be silenced. Enter nightclub owner Jack Ruby.

For millions of Americans, the shooting of Oswald by Ruby two days later was the final proof of a conspiracy. Yet the Warren Commission insisted Ruby had acted quite independently, that he impulsively walked into Dallas Police HQ at the precise moment Oswald was being led to a car to transfer him to jail and killed him to avenge Jackie Kennedy. That conclusion sounds even more feeble today than it did back then.

Soon after Oswald's arrest, Ruby had made a monumental number of telephone calls. And, like David Ferrie, he suddenly became flush with money. Though usually in debt, he was seen in his bank on the afternoon of the assassination carrying $7,000 in cash – quite a sum for a man with financial problems.

He also started showing an obsessive interest in Oswald. At 7pm that night he managed to open a door to the room where Oswald was being interrogated, and was told to move on by a policeman who knew him. Later that night he was present at a press conference at which Oswald was briefly paraded, and he was back again the next day trying to find out when Oswald was to be transferred.

It now seems certain he finally got his way by bribing a police officer to slip him past the heavy security at the crucial time.

But it is Ruby's background, glossed over by the Warren Commission, that adds a sinister twist. He was, in fact, a minor figure in the Mafia who, according to FBI documents, had for years been a 'pay-off man for the Dallas Police Department'. But the man to whom he was probably ultimately responsible was Mafia boss Carlos Marcello.

Ruby maintained until his death in jail in 1967 of cancer that he had been framed into killing Oswald. But at least he died peacefully – others involved were not so lucky.

One of the features of the assassination is the chain of murders, accidents and apparent suicides left in its wake. Apart from Oswald himself, and men like David Ferrie and his associate Eladio del Valle, many key witnesses died suddenly and violently.

Three newspaper reporters who spoke to Ruby about the Kennedy case also died in rapid succession, one from a gunshot wound, one from a karate chop and the other from a drug overdose. Three Mafia men were murdered shortly after a new government inquiry team asked to see them. Another important witness was found shot dead two hours after learning that congressional investigators wanted to question him about his links with Oswald.

The House Select Committee on Assassinations finally came up with its findings – several theories, but few conclusions – in 1979. One theory to which they gave strong credence was that Kennedy's death was a direct result of his Cuban policy.

Following the 1961 Bay of Pigs invasion in which exiled anti-Castro Cubans, trained by the CIA and backed by Kennedy, landed on Cuba in a disastrously bungled coup attempt, the severely embarrassed president slowly began soft-pedalling in his attitude to Castro. By 1963, in the wake of the Cuban missile crisis, he was making it clear he wanted operations against Castro stopped. The anti-Castro Cubans were furious – furious enough, some think, to turn against Kennedy and plot to kill him.

Here, they might have found willing allies in men like Marcello and his fellow crime boss Santos Trafficante, whose lucrative gambling and prostitution empire in Cuba had crumbled after Castro's takeover.

Both Marcello and Trafficante loathed John Kennedy and his brother Robert. Both were suffering under the relentless crusade against organised crime initiated by Robert Kennedy, as attorney general, with Jack's blessing. The Kennedy brothers were pursuing the Mafia as never before, and a multibillion dollar empire was becoming seriously threatened.

To his undying fury, Marcello was deported on Robert Kennedy's orders. On his return, say associates, the proud Sicilian swore revenge. One chilling conversation between Marcello and three colleagues in late 1962 was described to the House Select Committee on Assassinations. Referring to the Kennedys, he said: 'The dog will keep biting you if you only cut off its tail.' He clearly believed that with John Kennedy dead, Robert Kennedy would cease to be attorney general – a correct prediction. He even spoke of 'setting up a nut to take the blame'. It was at about this time too that Trafficante reportedly told an associate: 'The president is going to be hit.'

In 1979 the committee felt sufficiently confident to declare that elements of the Mafia were behind Kennedy's killing. It added that 'the most likely family bosses of organised crime to have participated were Carlos Marcello and Santos Trafficante,' both of whom had motive, means and opportunity.

But as with every other theory into the vilest assassination of the century, there was no proof. The murder of John Fitzgerald Kennedy remains one of the murkiest mysteries of all time.

JACK THE RIPPER

Jack the Ripper is hardly the most prolific murderer in the annals of crime. This Victorian killer put paid to no more than five humble prostitutes. Yet his brief reign of terror has become perhaps the most tantalising murder mystery of all time. In fact, the story of Jack the Ripper raises two mysteries – the first being his identity, the second being why his notoriety has continued to fascinate us for more than a century.

To historians, forensic experts and amateur sleuths worldwide, the dastardly deeds of Jack the Ripper have become the greatest unsolved and intriguing series of bloody atrocities in criminal history. Since his skilled slayings shocked England in 1888, researchers have endlessly poured over the few, juicy clues that he left behind. And rather than interest in him waning, investigation is again intensifying, guaranteeing the vile perpetrator a place in history.

Although particularly gory (each killing was followed by mutilation with surgical precision) the Ripper's brief crime wave was quickly forgotten after the turn of the century. Yet, in recent years books galore have been written about him. Speculation as to his identity is rife and often wildly wide of the mark – which has resulted in Jack being credited with many more names than the number of his victims!

Was the murderer a self-styled purger of

prostitutes who plied their sad trade under the gaslights of London's East End? Was he a Jewish ritual slaughterman, as some clues suggested? Was he a surgeon who had turned his talents to butchery? Was he a mortician, skilled in the art of disembowelling? Was he a policeman, his nightly beat giving him the perfect alibi to be out on those dark, dank streets? Was 'he' in fact a 'she' – a midwife with a grudge? Or, most extraordinarily of all, was the killer a deranged member of the British royal family?

Amid this endless debate, it is easy to forget that Jack the Ripper's reign of terror was short and swift. It lasted less than three months. Between 31 August 1888 and 9 November 1888, five prostitutes were murdered. Then, just as suddenly as the slayings started they stopped.

Jack's first victim was Mary Ann Nichols, a 42-year-old prostitute who plied her trade in the Whitechapel area of the East End. 'Pretty Polly', as she was known, approached a tall stranger with the invitation: 'Looking for a good time, mister?' If the stranger had accepted, a sum of four pence would have exchanged hands and Mary would have spent it in one of the gin palaces that infested the area.

Instead, the man put his hands around her throat to stop her crying out, then dragged her into the darkness of an alleyway. Within seconds he had cut her from ear to ear.

A police surgeon who examined the body said: 'Only a madman could have done this. I have never

Many newspapers at the time of Jack the Ripper's reign of terror in the East End of London ran satirical cartoons depicting the police's inability to catch the murderer.

seen so horrible a case. She was ripped about in the manner only a person skilled in the use of a knife could have achieved.'

The residents of Bucks Row, where Mary Ann Nichols's body was found, were so ashamed of their sudden notoriety – and so outraged by officials who dubbed the street 'Killer Row' – that they petitioned to have it renamed. It was duly retitled Durward Street and remained so until it was demolished many years later.

Police put Mary's murder down to one single, frenzied attack. Then, a week later, on 8 September, another prostitute, 47-year-old 'Dark Annie' Chapman was butchered in Hanbury Street, near Spitalfields Market. Her few pitiful possessions had been laid out neatly alongside her disembowelled corpse. Also alongside her were her entrails, slashed out of her in a sexual frenzy.

A witness who dashed to the scene after hearing the cry 'Murder' said: 'I jumped off my cart, being a lad, and joined the crowd – and there she was, all her entrails steaming hot.'

Shortly afterwards a Fleet Street news agency received the following letter:

'Dear Boss, I keep on hearing that the police have caught me. But they won't fix me yet. I am down on certain types of women and I won't stop ripping them until I do get buckled. Grand job that last job was. I gave the lady no time to squeal. I love my work and I want to start again. You will soon hear from me with my funny little game. I saved some of the proper stuff in a little ginger beer bottle after my last job to write with but it went thick like glue and I can't use it. Red ink is fit enough, I hope. Ha, ha. Next time I shall clip the ears off and send them to the police, just for jolly.'

The Ripper's third victim was 44-year-old Elizabeth 'Long Liz' Stride. Her body was found in Berner Street, Whitechapel, on 30 September. Police believe the killer had been disturbed in his grisly work because, although the victim's throat had been cut, her body was otherwise untouched.

Victim number four was discovered on the same day not far away in Mitre Square. This time the Ripper achieved the bestial satisfaction he seemed to crave. Catherine Eddowes, a drunkard in her forties who had just been released from police cells after causing an affray, was disembowelled and her intestines draped across her right shoulder. Her face had been hacked off and her ears were missing.

A trail of blood led from Catherine's corpse to a torn part of her apron. And on a nearby wall was scrawled in chalk: 'The Jewes (sic) are not men to be blamed for nothing.'

The Ripper's final victim was Mary Kelly, younger than her predecessors at just 25 years of age. Mary, also a prostitute, had accosted a man on the night of 9 November. He was described as being tall, dark, with a moustache and a deerstalker hat.

Poor Mary was butchered not in the street but in her own tiny apartment, where the Ripper spent hours grotesquely mutilating her. The following morning her landlord knocked on her door to demand his rent. After discovering her remains, he told police: 'I shall be haunted by this sight for the rest of my life.'

Terror had by now gripped the East End. Vigilante groups were formed and a host of accusations were bandied about. Was the Ripper a mad surgeon? Was he a Jewish ritual slaughterman, as the writing on the wall seemed to suggest? Was he a policeman on his nightly rounds, his job giving him the perfect alibi to be out on the streets?

One suspect was revealed by Inspector Robert Sagar, who played a leading part in the investigation. Shortly before his death in 1924, Sagar said:

'We had good reason to suspect a man who lived in Butcher's Row, Aldgate. We watched him carefully. There was no doubt this man was insane. After a time his friends thought it was advisable to have him removed to a private asylum. Once he was removed, there were no more Ripper atrocities.'

After the slaying of poor Mary, London held its breath. The populace awaited news of another 'orrible murder'. But it never came. The killings had ended as suddenly as they had begun.

The Ripper fever died down – for half a century. Then, for some reason, fascination with the case slowly began to grow again. The pursuit of the Ripper's identity became a fresh fascination for modern-day criminologists. Today, with most of the crumbling old workers' homes gone and the taverns replaced with office blocks, the East End is a lurid shrine for Ripper enthusiasts. Americans are escorted on guided tours of the streets where the maniacal Jack dispensed with his victims, and sip beer afterwards in a pub named after him. Books are churned out and TV documentaries made, all posing the same question: Just who was Jack the Ripper? And all coming up with different answers...

The suspect favoured by several authors of Ripper investigations is Montagu John Druitt. In their book *The Ripper Legacy*, authors Martin Howells and Keith Skinner say that Druitt, an impoverished barrister, had been trained in medical skills as a young man. He was unstable and his family had a history of mental illness. His body was found floating in the Thames a few weeks after the murder of Mary Kelly.

Richard Gordon, famous for his 'Doctor in the House' series of comic novels, was an anaesthetist before turning to writing. In 1980 he retraced Jack's steps through the East End and observed:

'The victims died by having their throats cut. The vein in the neck is only three or four inches from the heart and, given that the victim is apprehensive, the heart would be pumping at enormous pressure. It always does when you're frightened. That meant the villain chloroformed his victims first, because that slows down the heartbeat.'

For this reason, said Richard Gordon, the Ripper was not only a doctor but an anaesthetist like himself.

The most original theory, however, came from author William Stewart who suggested that Jack was really Jill the Ripper, a midwife and abortionist who went mad after serving a jail sentence for prostitution.

Almost unbelievably, another suspect was a member of the British royal family. Suspicion fell on Queen Victoria's grandson, Prince Eddy – or, to give him his full title, Albert Victor Christian Edward, duke of Clarence and Avondale, heir to the throne and great uncle of the present queen.

Certainly the talk at the time was that the prince was a bisexual who had turned criminally insane after contracting venereal diseases. According to renowned forensic psychiatrist Dr Harold Abrahamsen in his book *Murder and Madness: The Secret Life of Jack the Ripper*, the prince was supposedly aided and abetted in his dark deeds by his mentor, tutor and woman-hating homosexual lover James Stephen.

Prince Edward died in 1892 of brain damage brought on by syphilis, although the official report described his fatal ailment as pneumonia.

Excitement among Ripper hunters was rekindled in 1993 when a diary was said to have been discovered under floorboards of a house in Liverpool, proving that wealthy cotton broker James Maybrick was the killer. The discovery was enough to fire up one publishing house, but the claims and the diary itself were derided by experts.

The principal expert contracted by one newspaper to disprove the diary's authenticity was author Melvin

Harris, who himself has written one of the best researched books on the subject. In *The True Face of Jack the Ripper*, Harris names as his prime suspect Robert D'Onston Stephenson, born 20 April 1841, the son of a wealthy Hull mill owner.

As a youth, Stephenson became obsessed with witchcraft and, in his own word, the 'black arts'. He embarked on a tour of Europe, ending up in southern Italy, where in 1860 he joined Garibaldi's uprising as a medical officer. There he learned a further art – crude field surgery. He revelled in the adventure and particularly the butchery. Once the war was over, Stephenson sailed to West Africa where, he boasted later, he killed a black woman in cold blood because he believed she was a witch doctor.

Returning to Hull in 1863, he took a post as a customs officer but began resorting with prostitutes, contracted venereal diseases and was banished from home. He left in disgrace for London where, to spite his parents, he married their illiterate serving girl and changed his first name to Roslyn.

Author Melvin Harris believes that Mrs D'Onston Stephenson, who disappeared in 1887, was butchered by her husband. From wife murder, it was but a short step to the killing of the five Whitechapel prostitutes the following year. The devious Stephenson then became a self-professed expert on the crimes and persuaded the *Pall Mall* magazine to publish his articles, which examined the slayings with a strange authority and detail.

In his later years, Stephenson experienced a religious conversion and, seemingly by way of atonement, wrote a tortuous study of the earliest translations of the Gospels. He completed his book in 1904 and thereafter vanished without trace. No death certificate for him has ever been found – leaving yet another mystery for the 20th-century detectives seeking the true identity of Jack the Ripper.

JACK THE STRIPPER

Jack the Ripper may well have been the first and most notorious murderer who we would now brand as a serial killer. But although the activities of his near-namesake Jack the Stripper are less well known, the latter was equally adept at bringing terror and hysteria to the streets of London.

There are close parallels between these two maniacs. Firstly, they both targeted prostitutes. Secondly, they received sexual kicks out of the act of killing, an act which in both cases was peculiarly horrific. Thirdly, and most important of all, neither was ever caught!

The Stripper murders began in 1964, a full 76 years after the horrors unleashed in the East End. All were concentrated within a few miles of each other in West London and, though it remains unclear exactly how many were the work of the same man, police suspect the tally was at least six. By the time the third nude body was found, the effect on the public was verging on panic. Most women vowed to stay at home after dark until the monster was caught.

The first possible Stripper victim was a prostitute called Elizabeth Figg, dragged out of the Thames on 17 June 1959. She had been manually strangled, a mode of death which does not precisely conform to the Stripper's usual method of dispatch. Nevertheless, some detectives still believe Lizzie Figg was his first known victim.

Another possible early victim was Hannah Tailford, aged 30, who sometimes used the pseudonyms Ann Tailor, Theresa Bell or Hannah Lynch. She had also died from drowning in a West London stretch of the Thames (at least, that was the medical cause of death). After her body was recovered on 2 February 1964, police were told that she had been clinically depressed and they immediately suspected suicide. A pathologist put them right, however, when he discovered that her stomach contained remnants of a large undigested meal. In his experience, suicides did not indulge in feasts first.

The recovery of another nude prostitute's body from the Thames on 8 April began to sound alarm bells with senior Scotland Yard detectives. But, as yet, there was no obvious link between the young woman, 26-year-old Irene Lockwood, and Tailford. And the Figg case was too far in the past for a connection to be made.

Prostitution is well known as the oldest profession. It is also among the most dangerous. There was nothing particularly unusual about two prostitutes being murdered in London within ten weeks of each other. Besides, Lockwood's death may not even have been murder.

On the morning of 24 April, however, police attitudes hardened. A groundsman at a sports ground in Acton found the naked body of a young woman lying on some rubbish. Her name was Helene Barthelemy, she was aged 22 and she was a prostitute. She had been choked to death.

Unlike the other unfortunate young women, Barthelemy's body did yield some forensic clues. Her skin showed up microscopic traces of metallic paint, the type used for spraying cars. There were heat marks on one side of the body suggesting it had been stored close to some kind of transformer. Perhaps the killer had kept the corpse in a garage to await disposal. A team of officers from Shepherd's Bush police station was assigned to check the thousands of backstreet paint spray workshops in the city.

There were other sinister forensic discoveries. Four teeth had been knocked out of Barthelemy's mouth with considerable force, one of which had remained lodged in her throat. And one of her last acts on earth had clearly been to perform fellatio on a man; traces of sperm were recovered from the back of her mouth. Over the following months, the clues from this woman's death surfaced again in the murders of three more prostitutes.

The next victim was found on 14 July at 5.30am, her nude body bizarrely arranged on a garage forecourt with legs crossed and chest slumped forward. Forensic tests showed that Mary Fleming, from Notting Hill, had tiny flecks of car paint on her skin and sperm traces in the back of her throat. Her false teeth were missing.

Fleming had been asphyxiated; in other words her

killer had not put his hands around her neck to choke her, rather he had stopped her air supply by other means. Detective Superintendent John Du Rose, who as one of Scotland Yard's finest would later be put in charge of the enquiry, likened it to the effect of pushing a small apple into the back of the throat. He was being coy. The Stripper murdered his victims during fellatio by thrusting his penis into their mouths, while gripping their hair to prevent escape.

On 25 November police discovered that he had struck again. The body of a prostitute called Margaret McGowan, missing for almost a month, turned up on a rubbish dump off Horton Street, Kensington. Again there were the telltale clues – asphyxia, a dislodged tooth, sperm in the throat and flecks of paint on the skin. Margaret had also been an acquaintance of both Helene Barthelemy and Mary Fleming.

McGowan attracted additional media interest, however, because of her links with high-class procurers in the London sex market. Through them, the press uncovered a connection with characters on the edge of the John Profumo-Christine Keeler political sex scandal.

The Stripper's last victim was discovered on 16 February 1965 in bushes alongside an industrial estate in Acton. The body had been kept so close to heat it was almost mummified. Forensic examination confirmed that Bridget O'Hara had lost several teeth, had sperm in her throat and metallic paint on her skin. She bore all the trademarks of the murderer.

As public hysteria mounted, detectives were despatched to interview as many prostitutes as possible. Officers wanted descriptions of any clients with a penchant for violent oral sex. As Du Rose took formal control of the inquiry, pressure on the police to catch their man was growing intense.

Du Rose had an enviable reputation and his arrival brought what every murder squad desperately needs – a slice of luck. The body of O'Hara had been dumped almost on the killer's doorstep. The estate contained a spraypaint shop from which airborne flecks of paint were carried to the site of a transformer. Detectives questioned all 7,000 people who worked on the site, for by now Du Rose was certain one of them was the killer. He urged his men to be particularly thorough when questioning night workers because it seemed Jack the Stripper dumped the bodies of his victims under cover of darkness.

Yet still there was no breakthrough. Du Rose decided to try and flush the victim out with the help of newspapers. He called a press conference at which he claimed the hunt had been narrowed down to 20 suspects. A little later, the number of suspects had been halved. Finally, he bluffed his way through a statement announcing that only three names were left in the frame.

The psychological pressure on the murderer must have been severe. The death of O'Hara was the last killing, and although no one was brought to justice, Du Rose claimed that he had a prime suspect.

In his memoirs *Murder Was My Business*, John Du Rose gave a fascinating insight into the mind of a serial killer. He said that the first of the Stripper's killings may have been an accident. By choking the prostitute with his penis during orgasm, it could have been argued that he was guilty only of manslaughter. But Du Rose added: 'When he continued to indulge in his particular perversion, well knowing that the girls concerned would die, he must have recognised that he was fulfilling himself as a murderer.'

A month after the murder of Bridget O'Hara, a night security guard on the Acton industrial estate gassed himself with the exhaust from his own van. The bachelor, in his mid-forties, left a note saying: 'I cannot stand the strain any longer.'

In his memoirs, Detective Superintendent Du Rose made it clear that the man who took his own life was a prime suspect. He added: 'Because he was never arrested or stood trial, he must be considered innocent – and will therefore never be named.'

Had Du Rose 'got his man' by a police version of psychological warfare? What is true is that after the death of the security guard, there were no more Stripper-style murders.

THE *HINDENBURG* DISASTER

The *Hindenburg* was the most opulent form of transatlantic air travel ever known. She was the largest, most luxurious dirigible ever built. The splendour of her state rooms were matched by the spacious lounge, bar and dining room, in which meals and wines of surpassing excellence were served by chefs and waiters trained in Europe's finest establishments. There was even a lightweight piano, specially made from aluminium, to entertain the pampered passengers.

This graceful, cigar-shaped floating palace made her maiden flight in 1936 and swiftly became a travelling showpiece of Hitler's Germany. She was a symbol of Aryan superiority and a statement to the world that the age of the airship was here to stay.

The *Hindenburg* (the airship was named after one of Germany's greatest generals) made a number of flights to the United States and even to Brazil during her first year in service. These runs went without a hitch. Throughout 1936 and early 1937, she glided effortlessly from her base at Frankfurt across the Atlantic and back under the expert command of Max Pruss, a seasoned Zeppelin commander.

On 3 May 1937 she was again launched from her mooring tower at Frankfurt on a scheduled flight to the United States. Carrying 36 passengers, she was only half full, although the return flight was fully booked. Along with the crew, the full complement aboard totalled 97.

The lack of fare-paying passengers on this transatlantic trip had nothing to do with fear. Despite the crash of the British airship *R101* seven years earlier, travel by dirigible was viewed as being utterly safe – which indeed it should have been.

The *Hindenburg* could have flown on harmless helium, but the only nation producing sufficient quantities of it in those days was the United States – and they withheld exporting it to Hitler's Germany as war clouds gathered over Europe in case it was used for his military machine. So the airship's 16 huge gas cells were instead filled with highly inflammable hydrogen. Even so, there was no reason to fear for the safety of the mighty ship.

Inside the *Hindenburg*, there were sophisticated insulation devices and warning systems to detect any leakages of gas. All crew members wore anti-static, asbestos-impregnated overalls and shoes soled with hemp. All crew members had to hand in matches and lighters before embarking, as did all passengers. If guests wished to smoke they were seated in a special pressurised lounge. A steward performed the function of lighting their cigars or cigarettes in another room, sealed off by a double door.

The safety standards were of the highest because the vessel had a proud record to live up to; there had never been a fatality in German civil airship travel. Yet

The above image is engraved in many people's minds.
However, what is not always remembered about the
Hindenburg disaster is the political intrigue involved.

the *Hindenburg* was to the skies what the *Titanic* was to the seas. She excelled in grandeur and style, and boasted every safety feature of her age. But, just like the great ship, which was doomed to die on an Atlantic crossing, the *Hindenburg* met her end after crossing the ocean, transformed in seconds from a traveller's heaven into a burning hell.

The fateful crossing had taken longer than anticipated. A headwind had delayed the airship by ten hours, and it was already 3.30pm on 6 May when the floating palace passed above Manhattan's Empire State Building in a show of graceful one-upmanship by the Germans over their American rivals. It also provided a spectacular treat for the 36 passengers.

Because of rain, wind and cloud conditions, coupled with poor visibility, Commander Pruss further delayed the flight and it was not until 7pm that the *Hindenburg* approached her final destination: Lakeheath naval station, New Jersey. The mooring ropes were dropped at 7.25pm

A radio reporter, Herbert Morrison, who was watching the darkened sky with studied indifference, took up the story.

'The ropes have been dropped and they have been taken hold of by a number of men in the field. The back motors of the ship are holding it just enough to keep it...'.

Here Morrison suddenly stopped, momentarily lost for words. Before his very eyes, the unthinkable was happening. Within seconds of the guide ropes being lowered for landing, flames erupted from the body of the great airship. The *Hindenburg,* filled with 98,000 cubic metres / 257,400 cubic yards of highly inflammable hydrogen, was gutted by fire.

Radio reporter Morrison was dumbstruck only for a moment. He continued to broadcast what he saw of the tragic event live to the American nation. His emotional speech has since gone down in history. In a voice becoming increasingly stricken with the horror of the scene, he went on:

'It's burst into flame! This is terrible... the flames are 500 feet into the sky... it is in smoke and flames now, those passengers... I'm going to have to step inside where I can't see it. I... I... folks, I'm going to have to stop for a while. This is the worst thing I've ever witnessed. It is one of the worst catastrophes in the world.'

These were the choked words uttered by the voice of Morrison as he described the death of *Hindenburg.* Other eyewitnesses recall the belly of the ship glowing red before sheet flame broke from the tail. The night air was filled with the hissing of the fire as it gorged itself hungrily on the gas-filled ship. Explosions could be heard up to 24km / 15miles away as, one by one, the giant gas bags exploded.

It was a nightmarish scene as passengers and crewmen jumped from windows and doors while the ship thrashed in her final agony.

Commander Pruss stayed at his controls in the command gondola until the ship hit the ground. He survived but his first captain, Ernst Lehmann, was mortally injured. He was found crouching in the glowing rubble, mumbling over and over: 'I don't understand, I don't understand.'

The airship had gone up in a mere 32 seconds from a cause unknown. Miraculously though, 62 of the 97 passengers and crew lived. Twenty crewmen and 15 passengers were killed.

An official inquiry was set up to pinpoint the cause of the disaster. Their very first suspicion was sabotage, and every surviving member of the crew was questioned along these lines. Suddenly and mysteriously, however, the sabotage theory was dropped and other factors were considered: engine sparks, leaky gas valves and static electricity. But none proved conclusive.

The inquiry finally settled on a rare form of static electricity, called St Elmo's fire, as being the likely cause. St Elmo's fire has been witnessed on the masts of ships at sea, on aircraft propellers and around trees. It glows like a flame during stormy weather and, for want of something to pin the disaster on, the inquiry opted for it.

The verdict instantly drew fierce criticism from scientists, who said it could not possibly be the cause of the inflagration because the hydrogen was far too tightly sealed for such a brief spark to ignite it.

Many observers suspected a cover-up to help maintain diplomatic relations between Germany and the United States. The German ambassador in

Washington had received a letter warning that a bomb was on the *Hindenburg*. It was only one of hundreds of anti-Nazi protests against visits by the airship – and indeed by conventional ships. The German liner *Bremen* had recently been boarded by demonstrators when it docked at New York. Security at the Manhattan liner berths and at Lakeheath had only just been stepped up accordingly.

The US government was even rightly concerned that the *Hindenburg* could be the target of snipers atop skyscrapers as it floated across the Manhattan skyline on its route to the naval station in Lakeheath, New Jersey.

There was also fear of sabotage on the German side. Opponents of the Nazis had threatened the airship in Frankfurt and security was also tight there. On the day of the flight, the Luftwaffe's new chief of special intelligence, Colonel Fritz Erdmann, was summoned to Berlin. There SS Stürmbannführer Kurt Hufschmitdt told him that a bomb had been defused aboard the *Hindenburg*'s sister-ship, the *Graf Zeppelin*. The suspect's deserted Frankfurt hotel room had been searched by the Gestapo who found detailed drawings of the *Graf Zeppelin* – and the *Hindenburg*. SS Stürmbannführer Kurt Hufschmitdt told Erdmann:

'We have reliable information that an attempt will be made to destroy your flight. The sabotage will come by bomb, probably after the airship has arrived over American soil. The attack is designed to make the Fatherland look vulnerable in the eyes of our enemies – disloyal Germans, Jews, and troublemakers in the United States.'

It was not until after the Second World War that other sinister evidence about the *Hindenburg* began to emerge. It was revealed that Luftwaffe chief Hermann Goering had issued a directive not to probe too deeply into the causes of the disaster. Was it because he did not want the pride of Nazi Germany dented still further by revelations that the airship was destroyed by a saboteur?

Then, 35 years after the disaster, author Michael Mooney added to the mystery. He said that three times during the flight a known communist sympathiser called at the airship company's offices to ask about the ship's position. Mooney put the blame for the blaze on a crew member – rigger Eric Spehl. Four simple facts, said Mooney, pointed to him being the saboteur.

First, Spehl's girlfriend was a fervent anti-Nazi who could have put him up to the plot. He had unhindered access to the bowels of the ship. At the time of the blast he had moved as far away from the seat of the fire as possible; he was right at the nose of the ship. Finally, two surviving crewmen said that before the blast they saw a flash going off, just like a photographer's bulb. Spehl was a photographer who had taken his camera onto the ship.

The true culprit may never be known, for Spehl died in the inferno. What also died that day was the dream of gracious and glamorous intercontinental air travel. The dreadful demise of the *Hindenburg*, coming only seven years after the crash of the British airship the *R101*, finally rang the death knell for these beautiful and silent leviathans of the sky.

MURDER ON MOUNT ACONCAGUA

It was an ambitious goal by anyone's standards – to climb a continent's highest mountain in the worst month of the year, when fierce weather would combine with the dangers of the peak to create an unassailable, formidable obstacle. Nevertheless, a team of eight amateur mountaineers were determined to conquer the slopes of Mount Aconcagua in Argentina, a 6,961 m /22,837ft monster renowned among climbers as being both dangerous and deadly.

It was in the summer of 1972 that two friends – Janet Johnson, a teacher, and John Cooper, an engineer – rallied together six other climbers to discuss an assault on the peak. The others, all from Colorado, were: team leader Carnie Defoe, a lawyer by profession; John Shelton, a doctor; William Zeller, a police officer; Arnold McMillen, a farmer; William Eubank, a geologist and James Petroske, a psychologist.

The group had climbed before and were fairly experienced. But the month they chose for the expedition earned them the scorn of local people and the advice of other climbers to abandon the project until better weather.

They had selected January the following year. January in the Andes is a bitterly cold month, plagued by driving snow, biting frosts and high winds. It is a time when even the natives living in the nearest town, Mendoza, barely venture out from their homes except for water and firewood. Nevertheless, Carnie Defoe, who had climbed extensively in Europe and the United States, persuaded the team they could do it.

It was an added element of the challenge – not only to conquer a peak that was difficult to climb, but to do it in extremely adverse weather conditions. It was a perverse challenge that perhaps can only be truly understood by other experienced mountaineers and explorers.

The only concession they made to the warnings they had been given about climbing in such conditions was to hire a guide. It was one of the few wise moves they made on their fateful mission. They chose a local climber, Miguel Angel Alfonso, whose knowledge of the area and the vagaries of its climate dramatically increased their survival chances.

Finally, with the route mapped out and their equipment packed, the team buoyantly sallied forth on their mission to conquer Aconcagua. Alfonso was later to tell policemen investigating the foolhardy expedition: 'They were very confident, and I was being paid for a job. I didn't know when we set out that it was going to end up as it did.'

The going was deceptively easy at first, the bitter weather seemingly giving way to a mild spell. But within a week the first of the party were beginning to show signs of fatigue. The higher they climbed, the colder the weather became, and the terrain grew steadily more treacherous.

At about 5,000m/16,404ft up the mountainside, Defoe and Shelton dropped out, suffering from frostbite and severe facial pains caused by the fierce winds. At 5,700m/18,700ft Eubank dropped out. The remainder plodded on, however, their strength ebbing quickly and morale desperately low. Only the mountain man Alfonso, who had grown up in this forbidding range of peaks, seemed to be little affected by the strain that was so telling on the party which he guided.

At 6,350m/20,833ft up the mountainside, Petroske was showing the telltale signs of mountain sickness: lightheadedness, vomiting and delirium. He was in such a bad way that Alfonso said it would be just a matter of hours before he lost the use of his limbs, and death would be certain because the weakened team would not have sufficient strength to carry him down the mountain.

Alfonso was asked to accompany him down to base camp and he agreed, reluctantly, because he did not relish leaving Johnson, Zeller, McMillen and Cooper alone on the peak. 'That was the last time I saw Janet and Cooper alive,' the guide was later to tell the police.

For what had begun as an adventurous climb ended as a double murder – the clues to which are shrouded in mystery to this day...

The party agreed to carry on as Alfonso stumbled

back down the mountainside with Petroske. For three days Alfonso and Petroske stayed sheltered from the atrocious weather in the base camp. Then the nightmare worsened. This is how Alfonso later told the story:

'I looked out of my window on the third day and saw figures in the distance. I left the cabin intending to help the others, but the weather forced me back. The next day I went out again and managed to reach them. I was shocked to find only Zeller and McMillen. I had assumed that the whole party had turned back, and therefore Johnson and Cooper should have been with them.

'Both men were in an awful state. Zeller had become blind because of frostbite and McMillen was bleeding heavily around his face, also because of frostbite. Both were totally disorientated, incoherent. They were muttering and shouting. They said things like, "Cooper is sitting near the paved road, near the trees" and that "Janet has been taken away by the women who came on mules."

'I took them back to the camp, where Petroske questioned them in his tent. I don't know what was said.'

What had happened on the terrible, wind-blown mountain slopes? Who were the women on mules? What was Cooper doing slumped by the trees near the paved road? No one to this day has been able to unravel the mystery.

An Argentinean climbing expedition later that

same year found the body of John Cooper. He had ice pick wounds to his stomach, but he had actually died from skull fractures caused by repeated blows to the head. Two years later the mountain yielded up the body of Janet Johnson, perfectly preserved in ice. She, too, had been beaten to death.

Police were unable to determine whether or not the pair had been attacked by some hardy band of mountain bandits. Or were the mules Zeller and McMillen had supposedly seen just an illusion brought on by their pain and misery?

Neither could police establish a motive for the killings. They had no money on them, nor was their practical mountain-climbing kit likely to attract the attention of anyone desperate enough for money to kill for it.

They died, and died horribly. But their case is unresolved, and looks like remaining so.

EARL OF ERROL

The rich pastures of Kenya's White Highlands were once nicknamed Happy Valley – not because of the region's natural beauty, but because of the privileged pleasures enjoyed by its wealthy inhabitants. In the days when Kenya was still a colony of the British Empire, Happy Valley was the setting for bawdy parties, drunken revelry, drug-taking and wild sex.

Even at the height of the Second World War, with Europe overrun by the Nazis, the champagne still flowed. More than 4,828km/3,000 miles away from war-torn England, the Happy Valley set, clustered around the Wanjohi River near Nairobi, could have been on a different planet. Holding court at the gracious Muthaiga Country Club, the flamboyant, drink-swilling, sexually licentious cocaine snorters were described by a contemporary writer as 'having libidos matched only by their unquenchable thirst for fine champagne, cognac and wines'.

Foremost among these hedonists was old Etonian Josslyn Victor Hay, 22nd earl of Erroll, Baron Kilmarnock, hereditary high constable of Scotland, known as the 'Passionate Peer' because of his amorous adventures. Hay, 39, was a suave philanderer and an accomplished seducer whose favourite catchphrase was: 'To hell with husbands.'

Despite having been expelled from Eton and later being cited in a divorce case in which the judge called him 'a very bad blackguard', Josslyn Hay had landed on his feet as an administrator of one of the jewels in Britain's colonial crown. He was a military secretary at a time when Kenya was an all-important strategic mustering point for British forces planning the assault on Ethiopia, then part of fascist Italy's pathetic East African empire. Hay's days were spent writing languid memos to London and his nights at the Muthaiga Club looking for fresh female challenges.

On the night of 30 November 1940 just such a challenge materialised in the lounge. She was a stunning ash-blonde beauty with an English rose complexion, and she entered the club with a man who was old enough to be her father. Hay made haste to introduce himself. He discovered that the old man was property magnate and racing fanatic Sir Henry Delves Broughton, known to his expatriate pals simply as 'Jock'. The beautiful young lady was his bride Diana Caldwell who, at 26, was 30 years younger than her husband. The couple had emigrated to Kenya a week after their wedding.

Josslyn Hay later told friends: 'Never can I remember a woman having such an immediate impact on me. I saw her eyes boring into me and I knew then that I must have her. I walked over to her while Jock was at the bar and said to her, "Well, who is going to tell Jock – you or I?".'

Diana was entranced by the master seducer. It was

Sir Henry Delves Broughton, although acquitted, never got over being charged with the murder of his young wife's lover.

not long before both became willing participants in a passion that would eventually lead to murder.

Sir Henry had struck an extraordinary pact with Diana, promising not to stand in her way if she fell in love with a younger man and to pay several thousand pounds annually to her for some years after their divorce. But he could hardly have been expected to realise that their marriage would founder within so short a time.

On 18 January Diana told Sir Henry that she was madly in love with Hay and reminded her husband of the promise of her freedom. Sir Henry offered to take her on a three-month trip to Ceylon – and that if she would reconsider her feelings on the journey, she could bring Hay along. Diana rejected the offer and two days later walked out on him, saying that she was going to live with Hay.

Three days later, Delves Broughton rang the police and reported a burglary, saying that two revolvers, some money and a cigarette case had been stolen. That same day he saw his lawyer about a divorce and later wrote to a close friend: 'They say they are in love with each other and mean to get married. It is a hopeless position and I'm going to cut my losses. I think I'll go to Ceylon. There's nothing for me to live in Kenya for.'

The following day he received an anonymous note, reading: 'There's no fool like an old fool. What are you going to do about it?'

As Diana moved into Hay's colonial mansion,

where they made love on silk sheets monogrammed with his family crest, some of Jock's friends, fearing for his emotional state, began to rally round and comfort him. One of these, a Mrs Carberry, invited him to tea on 23 January. Unfortunately, Diana and Hay turned up unexpectedly – part of the latter's wicked manoeuvrings aimed at making his mistress's husband suffer.

However, Jock's demeanour disappointed Hay at the tea. It was a set piece of English politeness, of stiff upper lips and no mention of broken hearts and betrayed passions. Afterwards, Lord Errol told a friend: 'Jock could not have been nicer. He has agreed to go away. As a matter of fact he has been so nice it smells bad.'

That night there was more largesse on the part of Delves Broughton. At a dinner party at the club, where by now everyone knew of the steamy affair, the cuckolded husband raised his glass in a toast and declared: 'I wish them every happiness. May their union be blessed with an heir. To Diana and Joss.'

At about 2am, slightly the worse for wear, having imbibed huge quantities of champagne, Delves Broughton returned to his house. Hay promised to deliver Diana safely home, and at 2.15am he dropped her off in his Buick.

At 3am on the morning of 24 January 1941 the native driver of a milk truck discovered the body of Josslyn Victor Hay slumped under the dashboard of his car, which had left the road and plunged into a ditch only 5km/3 miles from Delves Broughton's home. It was no accident – he had been shot through the head at point-blank range with a .32 revolver. Police were called and the local pathologist, who happened to be driving past the spot on his way to work, hauled the corpse from the car at 8am. He immediately recognised Hay.

Extraordinarily, it was only after Hay's burial on 25 January that the police announced he had been murdered. They said that someone had either flagged the car down, had been sitting beside the driver or had fired a shot through the open window from the running board.

Diana accused her husband of cold-bloodedly killing her lover out of jealousy. But for some reason she relented, and by the time police formally charged Delves Broughton with the murder, she had flown to Johannesburg to hire him top criminal lawyer Harry Morris. It was a worthwhile investment.

Morris called experts to prove that the three bullets fired at Josslyn Hay could not have come from any gun owned by Broughton. He also performed masterfully in the dock. Of the love trysts that happened under his own roof, he said :

'She could ask who she liked. I should not have tried to stop her in any event. I see no point in it. We met every day at the club and I cannot see it makes any difference if a man comes to stay the night. In my experience of life, if you try to stop a woman doing anything, she wants to do it all the more. With a young wife the only thing to do is keep her amused.'

On 1 July 1941 Delves Broughton was found not guilty of murdering Josslyn Victor Hay, 22nd Earl of Erroll. The file on the crime has never been closed because the murderer has never been caught. Was the killer Delves Broughton or another cuckolded husband? Was it one of Hay's previous mistresses – perhaps the beautiful American heiress Alice de Janze, who had shot dead a previous lover in Paris five years before? Or was it Diana herself, perhaps believing that the Passionate Peer was about to desert her just like all the lovers that had passed before?

Neither Diana nor her husband ever revealed the answer to the mystery. The old man took Diana to Ceylon as planned before returning to England, ailing and partially paralysed. He committed suicide in Liverpool on 5 December 1942, leaving notes which said he had found the strain of the trial and accompanying publicity too much to bear.

Diana returned to Kenya where she remained until her death in 1987, a rich, enigmatic, extravagant lady to the last.

DREYFUS

On the face of it, Captain Alfred Dreyfus seemed unlikely material for a spy. Yet when a seemingly incriminating note about military matters was fished from a wastepaper basket in a French Army barracks in September 1894, Dreyfus seemed to be the first name on everyone's lips.

The note, written on onion skin paper, mentioned five documents which were being sent under separate cover. They were to include details of a field gun and of artillery formations. The note – which ended with the words 'I am just going on manoeuvres' – was unsigned, but had obviously been written by an officer.

Since the piece of paper had been misappropriated from the wastepaper basket of Colonel Max von Schwarzkoppen, the prominent German military attaché in Paris, its meaning was clear to the French top brass – one of their brother officers was a traitor, spying for Germany.

On 26 September 1894, several senior officers were summoned to the War Ministry in Paris where intelligence officer Major Hubert-Joseph Henry showed them the note. Major Henry's superior, Colonel Jean-Conrad Sandherr, announced that he had ordered a hasty handwriting comparison and was utterly convinced the note belonged to Dreyfus. Major Henry's eager colleague, Major Du Paty de

Dreyfus is pictured here in front of the court martial at Rennes. This single man divided France between his right-wing detractors and his left-wing supporters.

Calm, ignominiously arrested the unfortunate Dreyfus, who cried out: 'I am going mad!'

Captain Alfred Dreyfus had already come to the attention of his superiors for his criticism of high-ranking army officers. Born in 1859, he came from a wealthy Jewish family, who had abandoned their home in Alsace when the Germans had taken control of the region. It was also a time when anti-Semitism was rife throughout France.

France was baying for blood when the trial of Dreyfus got underway in December 1894, having feasted on rumours and lies expounded by the French press. The hearing was held in secret, despite vigorous protests by Dreyfus's lawyer who wanted a trial in open court. The evidence against him was of the flimsiest but the verdict, after only three days trial, was predictable.

His penalty was deportation. Before that came the ritual humiliation of having his badges ripped from his uniform and his sword snapped in two. He was sent to the infamous *Ile du Diable*, Devil's Island, a former convicts' leper colony off the coast of French Guiana, which was used by France as a penal settlement until 1938. There Dreyfus faced years of solitary confinement, shackled to his bed at night with iron chains.

Dreyfus might have remained there had it not been for the intervention of Major Marie-Georges Picquart who, replacing Sandherr as France's chief spy-hunter, continued the investigation into supposed espionage efforts by German envoys in Paris. The difference was that Picquart was as honourable as Sandherr had been dishonest.

Into Major Picquart's hands fell a fresh piece of evidence. By good fortune, it emanated from the very same wastebin as the note that had damned Dreyfus. This time it was a torn-up postcard bearing a cryptic message and addressed to a Major Marie-Charles-Ferdinand Walsin Esterhazy. The finger of guilt suddenly pointed towards him.

Esterhazy was already known for his overt curiosity about army secrets. Furthermore, he was a long-time friend of the original complainant, intelligence officer Major Henry. When Picquart matched Esterhazy's handwriting to that on the original note, he knew immediately that a grave miscarriage of justice had been done. Yet when he presented his findings to his superior, General Boisdeffre, he was told to keep the two cases separate. In other words, abandon Dreyfus and his only hope of freedom.

Picquart was appalled. His reward for his honesty and integrity was a hazardous posting in rebellious French North Africa, where chances were that his cause – and he himself – was likely to die. He survived, however, and continued to agitate on behalf of Dreyfus even though it cost him his career.

Now what had started out as a straightforward case of espionage became a national cause célèbre between left-wing and right-wing political factions.

The unfortunate Captain Dreyfus remained festering on Devil's Island, stripped of his army rank. But back home in France, suspicions that he was no more than a fall guy for the state soon rent the country in two.

As months and years passed by, the aggrieved leftists continued to canvass their belief that the evidence against Dreyfus was fabricated and that the reason for his victimisation was merely because he was Jewish. The military hit back by producing three letters, which they claimed had just come to light and which proved Dreyfus's guilt once and for all. Immediately, Picquart branded one of the letters a forgery and pointed out that the other two simply did not refer to Dreyfus at all.

The man behind the forgery was at last forced to admit his role in the conspiracy. Predictably, he was none other than Major Henry. The next day, Henry was discovered dead in his prison cell having slit his own throat. Another man implicated in the scandal, by the name of Lemercier-Picard, hanged himself.

The cauldron of scandal was at boiling point, and by 1897 it boiled over when Mathieu Dreyfus, a tireless campaigner on behalf of his wronged brother, publicly branded Esterhazy a traitor. Now the public standing of the army was at stake.

Esterhazy demanded a court martial to clear his name. A hearing was held and, in a shameful cover-up, it did indeed appear to clear him. The anti-Dreyfus lobby were delighted, but the wronged prisoner's supporters were so infuriated that they finally resorted to violence. Mobs supporting each side rioted and fought on the streets.

The more vocal the support for Dreyfus, the more determined the right wing became to establish his guilt. With the government lining up with the army and the Roman Catholic Church against Dreyfus the conflict between the two opposing sides engulfed the entire country.

France's leading novelist, Emil Zola, became embroiled in the campaign to clear Dreyfus. In 1898 Zola published a devastating open letter to the government. Titled *J'Accuse*, it denounced ministers for their role in the scandalous affair. The government could not allow the challenge to go unanswered and prosecuted Zola for libel. He was sentenced to a year in jail and went into exile upon his release.

Hope for Dreyfus appeared to rise when in 1899 a new president, Emile Loubet, ordered a retrial. Yet the court at Rennes again found the accused guilty of espionage and sentenced him to 10 years in jail.

Dreyfus, still a young man but stooped and white-haired because of his tropical captivity, was by now weary of being used as a political football. On 19 September 1899, having suffered a nervous breakdown, he ceased fighting to clear his name. Instead he agreed to accept a pardon and was freed. In June 1900 the government introduced a face-saving bill to grant amnesty to all those involved in the Dreyfus saga.

It was an attempt at a diplomatic whitewash that

was bound to fail. The truth about the Dreyfus affair had still not been told. The depth of the conspiracy to pervert the course of French justice had not been plumbed and the ensuing cover-up had not been investigated. Henry was dead, Boisdeffre had resigned and Du Paty de Calm was in prison for forging documents in the case. Top-ranking army officials had been exposed as liars and France was left looking ridiculous in the eyes of the world. And yet the roll of dishonour of the guilty was not published – and never would be.

It wasn't until 1906 that a fresh inquiry announced there was not a shred of evidence against Dreyfus. He was reinstated in the army with the rank of major and invited back to the Ecole Militaire, the scene of his humiliation 11 years earlier, where he was awarded the Legion d'Honeur. A year later, Dreyfus resigned from the army in disgust – although he went back into uniform to fight for his country in the First World War.

Of the major players in this great unsolved mystery, Dreyfus's great champion Emile Zola had returned from exile at the turn of the century and had again become his most vehement campaigner. In 1902 he and his wife Alexandrine were found dead of carbon monoxide poisoning in their Paris home. It seemed their chimney had been deliberately blocked, probably by members of the anti-Dreyfus camp.

In June 1908 Dreyfus was at a ceremony in honour of his defender Zola when two shots were fired. He was slightly hurt. At the other end of a smoking revolver was journalist Sosthene Gregory, 65, who believed he had been striking a blow against 'Dreyfusism'. Ironically, Gregory was saved from the crowd by Dreyfus's own loyal brother, Mathieu.

Dreyfus's long-time supporter Picquart was rehabilitated and rose to the rank of brigadier-general. As for Esterhazy, he fled to England after being accused of defrauding a cousin. He could only get a job as a canned food salesman and died in obscurity in 1923.

Dreyfus himself died in 1935, as anti-Semitism again spread through Europe.

BUSTER CRABB

In a smoke-filled room at a secret address in South London, the retired naval officer refilled his whisky glass and listened languidly to the man whose true name he did not know, but whose purpose he discerned quite well.

Commander Lionel Kenneth Philip Crabb OBE, GM, RNVR (Retd), better known to hero worshipping schoolboys throughout Britain as 'Buster', was being briefed on a special job for British intelligence. If it came off, the West would gain valuable information about the latest in Soviet naval technology. If it went wrong ... but Buster, a war hero, could not contemplate failure. This mission, like the ones before, would be a piece of cake.

The Cold War was at its height. It was 1956 and the whole of Europe was a giant bazaar where secrets were traded, spies were swapped and people were bought and sold. Britain had set out its own stall in the espionage market, but there were many who felt that it was now the right time to start actually talking to the other side instead of stealing their secrets.

One of these was Prime Minister Sir Anthony Eden. He and several of his like-minded ministers decided to sponsor a goodwill visit to Britain by the Soviet Union's Party General Secretary Nikita Khrushchev and the Prime Minister Nikolai Bulganin, hoping to establish the dawn of a new era in East

Navy man Commander Lionel 'Buster' Crabb was valued by the British government for his diving expertise, which was used for clandestine operations.

West relations.

Months before the VIP party was due to arrive, Eden summoned his professional spymasters, the heads of MI5 and MI6, and ordered that under no circumstances were they to carry out any clandestine operation which might jeopardise the success of the visit. The spymasters hypocritically nodded their agreement and promptly ignored their orders. And that's when they called in Commander Lionel Kenneth Philip Crabb OBE, GM, RNVR (Retd), better known as Buster Crabb.

The previous year Buster had been approached by British naval intelligence with a view to carrying out an underwater reconnaissance of the Soviet battlecruiser *Sverdlov*, which had docked at Portsmouth on a goodwill visit. Crabb was the ideal man for the job; during the Second World War he had become something of a legend by removing enemy limpet mines from the hulls of British ships. These dangerous exploits had earned him the George Medal, the Order of the British Empire and the thanks of a grateful nation.

After the war, however, Buster became like a fish out of water. He tried various jobs before he eventually took up diving again, exploring old wrecks and testing equipment for the Royal Navy.

Thus it was that Buster, at the age of 45 and a heavy smoker and drinker, was called on by his country to examine the hull of the *Sverdlov*. His mission was to find out if she had been fitted with a new device, codenamed Agouti, that deadened the sound made by the ship's propellers, rendering it more difficult to detect by a submarine's radar.

Buster carried out the operation well. Now the spymasters wanted to use him again. Khrushchev and Bulganin were due to sail into Portsmouth Harbour in the cruiser *Ordzhonikidze*, sister ship to the *Sverdlov*. They would then travel by train to London for talks with Eden and other government ministers.

Buster's role would be a repeat of Operation Sverdlov – but if anything went wrong his activities would be disowned by British intelligence, since he was no longer officially a naval officer.

The eager Buster was not told that this operation had been expressly prohibited by the prime minister. His briefing officer also failed to inform him about the massive security surrounding the Soviet visit. Unlike the *Sverdlov*, the *Ordzhonikidze* would be crawling with watchful KGB agents. The head of the KGB himself, Colonel-General Ivan Serov, had taken personal command of the security arrangements.

On 17 April 1956, as the *Ordzhonikidze* berthed in Portsmouth Harbour flanked by a flotilla of Soviet destroyers, Buster caught the London to Portsmouth train with his fiancée Patricia Rose. She was to say later that during the journey the indiscreet Buster had told her exactly what he had been hired to do.

Pat returned on the next train to London while Buster wandered into town to meet an MI6 agent who had been assigned to help him. The pair then booked into separate rooms at the Sally Port Hotel on Old Portsmouth High Street, Buster even registering in his own name.

After breakfast the following morning, the two men strolled down to the dockyard, which was teeming with both Royal Navy and visiting Soviet sailors. Buster was a well-known character among military personnel. The famous diver's face would have been recognised by many on the quayside, and there can be little doubt that Soviet intelligence agents would have spotted him immediately.

Having made their reconnaissance, Buster and his MI6 companion returned to the hotel. Over drinks, Buster decided to make his dive at 7am the following day – no time was to be wasted.

As 19 April dawned, the two men presented themselves at the main security gates leading to the dockyard. They were allowed in and Buster went off to change into his diving gear. With a cheerful wave to his companion, he then slid quietly into the cold waters of Portsmouth Harbour and began swimming towards the giant Soviet cruiser, anchored some 274m/300yd off shore...

Commander Lionel Kenneth Philip 'Buster' Crabb was never seen alive on British soil again.

Buster's MI6 agent, later identified as a low ranking officer called Teddy Davies, waited patiently at the dockside. But as the hours wore on it became clear that something had gone terribly wrong. Eventually Davies gathered up Buster's clothes and headed quickly back to the hotel, where he settled their bills and removed all trace of Buster's belongings. Then he phoned his bosses at MI6 to break the bad news.

After the initial shock upon hearing that their unofficial escapade had backfired, the spymasters decided that the best course would be to sit tight and hope no one – least of all the prime minister – would find out. Perhaps Buster was somewhere at the bottom of Portsmouth Harbour. His body might not be found for weeks.

But that night the first lord of the admiralty, who was attending a London dinner in honour of the Soviet guests, was astonished when one of them turned to him and asked: 'What was that frogman doing near our ship this morning?'

The spymasters were now in deep water. Eden blew his top at the security services who had so flagrantly disobeyed his orders. The following morning a full-scale inquiry was launched.

As yet, news of the incident had not been leaked to the press, so an elaborate cover-up was put in motion. MI5, which had been called in to help clear up the mess, ordered the head of Portsmouth CID to go to the Sally Port Hotel and double-check that no clues remained as to Buster's brief stay. Detective Superintendent Stanley Lambert duly searched the hotel and, despite protests from the manager, ripped four pages out of the register.

Much to the relief of the spymasters, the Soviets

said nothing about the incident, which gave Eden some hope that his attempt at East-West détente might be working. But on 23 April at a dinner for Khrushchev given by the opposition Labour Party, MP George Brown (later Baron George Brown) so offended the Soviet leader with a remark about human rights that the guests set sail for Leningrad in a mood of anger and indignation. The visit had been a disaster. And the world at large did not yet know about Buster Crabb.

Only after the Soviet delegation had returned home, and nine days after Buster's disappearance, was his fiancée Pat Rose informed that he was missing. The following day the Admiralty issued a statement that the intrepid diver was missing presumed dead after a 'test dive in connection with trials of certain underwater apparatus'. The statement added that the tragedy had happened in Stokes Bay, some three miles along the coast from Portsmouth.

This did not for one minute fool the press, who quickly discovered the detective's ham-fisted attempt at destroying the evidence by ripping pages from the hotel register. It also struck them as odd that the Royal Navy had made no attempt to find Buster's body in Stokes Bay. Soon every newspaper was pointing to the disappearance.

The Soviets, still smarting, now decided to play their hand. They sent an official note to the Foreign Office in London stating that a frogman had indeed been seen in the water near their ships. They followed this up by cunningly leaking the contents of the note to the press.

The resulting story was the espionage mystery of the decade. What had really happened to brave Buster? Had he been shot by a Soviet sailor on watch? Had he been hauled out of the water and taken prisoner? Or had Buster really been a Soviet agent all the time and was even now eating caviar with his bosses in the Kremlin?

The Soviets were enjoying watching Whitehall wriggle. Now they delivered the coup de grace. The British Foreign Office had sent a note to Moscow, in confidence, apologising for the whole affair. It read:

'The frogman who, as reported in the Soviet note, was discovered from the Soviet ships swimming between the Soviet destroyers, was in all appearances Commander Crabb. His presence in the vicinity of the destroyers occurred without any permission whatsoever and Her Majesty's government expresses its regret for the incident.'

The Soviets promptly leaked the note to the British press. The result was a political furore. On 9 May, Prime Minister Eden was forced to make a statement to the House of Commons admitting that the original Admiralty announcement of Crabb's disappearance was a pack of lies and that Crabb had indeed been swimming around the Soviet ships – although, he stressed, without the authority or knowledge of the British government.

Eden, who had been made to grovel publicly, now

wanted revenge on the spymasters who had treated his authority with such contempt. He ordered a secret inquiry which put a rocket through the hallowed halls of MI6, claiming on its way the scalp of the department's chief, Major General Sir John 'Sinbad' Sinclair, who was forced into early retirement.

But the press and the public were still not satisfied. Where was Buster, dead or alive?

An answer emerged, rather too conveniently, some time later when a fisherman found the headless and handless body of a frogman off a sandbank 16km/10 miles from Portsmouth Harbour on 26 June 1957. A post mortem revealed a scar on the left knee which, an inquest heard, Buster had sustained while diving over some barbed wire. The coroner recorded an open verdict, but said he was satisfied the body was that of Crabb.

The body was buried at Milton Cemetery, Portsmouth, on 5 July 1957. The funeral was not accompanied by a Royal Navy guard of honour. Neither was it attended by Buster's fiancée Pat Rose. She later made it clear that she did not believe that the body was Buster's.

Over the following years she was to receive telephone calls from people claiming to be in contact with Crabb in the Soviet Union. One mystery man said he had seen Buster in the Black Sea area, another that he knew Buster was living happily in Vladivostok. On one occasion Pat was actually approached by a man at a London mainline station who produced a photograph of Crabb, but would not let her keep it. In desperation, Pat wrote an appeal to Khrushchev, but received no reply.

Several respected public figures supported the theory that Crabb was still alive. Among them was the former head of MI5, Sir Peter Sillitoe, who in 1961 said publicly that a dossier on Crabb's activities in the Soviet Union had been gathered by the security services. Members of Parliament tried unsuccessfully to raise the matter in the commons.

Another adherent to the theory was author J Bernard Hutton, who claimed to have received a Soviet dossier outlining Buster's life and career since his disappearance. It stated that after several years he had been promoted to the rank of commander in the Soviet Navy and continued to enjoy life to the full behind the Iron Curtain.

In 1990 Buster's old Royal Navy diving partner, Sydney Knowles, broke a 34-year silence to claim that Crabb had been recruited for the Russians by two traitorous British spymasters, now deceased. They were Sir Anthony Blunt, who was stripped of his title when revealed as a Soviet agent in 1979, and Sir Roger Hollis.

Ironically, it was the sacking of British security chiefs in the aftermath of the Crabb fiasco that propelled Hollis to even greater power. Only months after Buster's disappearance, traitor Hollis was appointed director-general of MI5!

The maverick Buster, it seems, had been

unwittingly at the centre of one of the most embarrassing episodes of espionage the British government has ever had to face.

SKYJACKER

It was Thanksgiving Day, 24 November 1971, and the quiet little man clutching a canvas bag close to his chest in the departure lounge of Portland Airport, Oregon attracted little attention. The airport was crammed with travellers anxious to get home to spend the holiday with their families.

The quiet man was among 150 passengers waiting patiently to take the 400-mile journey from Portland to Seattle, Washington. After acquiring a ticket under the name of D B Cooper, he entered the departure lounge and waited patiently behind his dark-tinted glasses. When he boarded the Boeing 727 50 minutes later, he was still clutching the canvas bag. He placed no luggage in the hold, requested an aisle seat from the stewardess and settled down with the bag on his lap apparently to enjoy the one-hour flight.

About halfway through the journey he pushed the overhead button to summon a stewardess. Tina Mucklow walked down the aisle ready to take his order for a drink, when the drama began.

Instead of giving her an order, he thrust into her hand a note reading: 'I have a bomb with me. If I don't get $200,000 I will blow us all to bits.'

As the startled employee of Northwest Airlines hurriedly digested the dire threat, Cooper opened the bag to show her a bomb; inside she saw clearly the dynamite sticks, wiring and detonator. He never took his eyes off her as he closed the bag and watched the woman walk up to the flight deck. Cooper sat back, awaiting the response.

The Boeing, like all modern aircraft susceptible to skyjacking, was equipped with a special device which broadcast over several frequencies the message that an emergency was underway. Within seconds of Tina blurting out her news to the flight deck crew, the switch was activated. Within two minutes it had been picked up by ground control at Seattle, where a team of FBI agents, police marksmen and units of the National Guard were mobilised and placed at strategic positions.

The plane landed uneventfully at the airport, where a message from the captain announced that disembarkation would be delayed. Amid the commotion of dismayed passengers, Cooper left his seat. Still clutching his canvas bag, he walked through the bulkhead door to the flight deck, where he confronted the pilot, copilot and flight engineer.

'Now gentlemen,' he said coolly, 'don't bother to look round.' There followed a tense 20-minute dialogue with air traffic control staff and then with a police chief, who asked for the release of the passengers before any bargains were struck.

The man was unequivocal in his demands. The passengers would be released only after $200,000 in used dollar bills had been handed over to him.

Cooper got his way, and two FBI agents dressed as

maintenance men wheeled a trolley aboard. Inside it was a white sack sealed with wire. Cooper ripped it open and found to his delight the money, together with the four parachutes he had also demanded. He then relented and allowed the passengers to leave.

Cooper moved into phase two of his bold plan when the passengers were all safely off the plane and in the terminal. He was now captor of the flight crew only, and made further demands to the police and airport authorities. He demanded that the plane be refuelled, and he warned that he wanted flight plans to take the aircraft to Mexico. In his exchanges with the ground staff, Cooper displayed a depth of knowledge about aircraft which indicated he was not a lucky amateur. This escapade had been plotted to keep it simple – brilliantly simple.

When the aircraft took off again, it was shadowed by a US Air Force fighter scrambled to track the plane to its final destination. Cooper seemed to sense the precautions that the authorities down below would take and, when airborne, told Captain Bill Scott that they were to alter course.

He was not to head for Mexico, but to veer south. He barked specific flying instructions at Scott, again indicating an astute knowledge of flying. He said: 'Fly with the flaps lowered, 15 per cent, keep the landing gear down, keep the speed below 90 metres per second, do not climb above 7,000 feet ... and open the rear door.'

The captain did some quick mental arithmetic

before telling Cooper that his instructions would mean a massive leap in fuel consumption. The skyjacker moved through the door from the cockpit to the body of the aircraft, and turned to say that the captain could land in Reno, Nevada. He told the captain to keep the bulkhead door locked.

As Cooper stood in the belly of the plane, there was a huge rush of air and a deafening roar as Captain Scott activated the mechanism opening the rear door, as demanded by his passenger...

Scott was not to know it until he landed at Reno nearly four hours later that, in the freezing night sky, shrouded by cloud and out of sight of the shadowing military planes, Cooper made his leap into the thin air. He left behind two parachutes, one intact, one in shreds. Investigators theorised later that he had ripped one apart to make a pouch for his loot that he strapped to his body. Examination of the flight's black box recorder showed a slight increase in height at the moment he jumped – the compensation for his weight and that of his ransom. The recorder showed that Cooper jumped at 8.13pm, just 32 minutes after leaving Seattle.

When the aircraft landed, the authorities became painfully aware that they had been well and truly duped. A contingency plan to storm the aircraft was rendered worthless when it was learned that Cooper had jumped. But they consoled themselves with the thought that the parachute jump was the one weak point in Cooper's expert plan. He had no winter clothes, no food and wore just lightweight shoes and a raincoat for protection. His pursuers took some solace in the firm knowledge that D B Cooper had baled out over rocky, mountainous, deeply wooded terrain that boasted sub-zero temperatures and dangerous wildlife.

There was little that could be organised in the way of a ground search over such hostile terrain. Federal aviation experts calculated that the odds on him surviving the leap in the dark were heavily stacked against him.

For two weeks after his vanishing act, exhaustive aerial searches covering vast tracts of land went on unabated. Planes with heat-seeking sensors and cameras crisscrossed the skyways over Oregon, Washington and Nevada. There was no sign of him. Army and airforce personnel joined in the ground searches, but it was all quite fruitless. Then, three weeks after the hijacking, the following letter arrived unexpectedly at the *Los Angeles Times* office:

'I am no modern-day Robin Hood. Unfortunately I have only fourteen months left to live. The hijacking was the fastest and most profitable way of gaining a few last grains of peace. I didn't rob Northwest because I thought it would be romantic, or heroic, or any other euphemisms that seem to attach themselves to situations of high risk.

'I don't blame people for hating me for what I've done, nor do I blame anybody for wanting me caught and punished, though this can never happen. I knew from the start I would not be caught. I have come and gone on several airline flights since and I'm not holed up in some obscure backwoods town. Neither am I a psychopath. I have never received a speeding ticket.'

Many of the 'mountain men' living in the region where Cooper jumped disregarded the letter, preferring to believe it was a spoof. Instead, they embarked on wild treasure hunts amid the peaks and valleys. Clubs organised 'Cooper Loot' hunt weekends, and it became fashionable for families to spend the weekends barbecuing in the mountains with a little light treasure hunting thrown in.

The authorities harnessed the latest technology to try to trace the money and/or Cooper's remains. Despite the letter, many high-ranking federal agents, accepting the evidence of the experts, could not believe that he survived the leap. One year after the skyjack, the FBI publicly announced that they thought D B Cooper dead.

Five years after the crime, on 24 November 1976, the file was closed on him, and the statute of limitations meant that even if he were alive, he was a free man. The only crime he could possibly be convicted for after that was tax evasion!

In 1979 a deer hunter out on a dawn walk in the Kelso Forest discovered the plastic warning sign of a Boeing 727 rear door hatch. It read: 'This hatch must remain firmly locked in flight.' The discovery was akin to gold being struck in the Klondike. Treasure-seekers from all over America poured into the nearest village. In their wake came map makers, astrologers and souvenir sellers who certainly got far richer than the luckless prospectors, who scoured the forests and mountains in vain for the Cooper Loot.

It was not until seven years after the crime that painter Harold Ingram and his eight-year-old son Brian made a discovery which many believe proves conclusively that Cooper died in his spectacular jump. They found $3,000 near a riverbank, and experts calculated that it had probably been washed down to the tranquil picnic spot by a mountain stream. The money was conclusively identified by the serial numbers as being Cooper's haul.

The Ingrams' discovery sparked a new wave of treasure fever. This time a group calling itself the 'Ransom Rangers' set out to try to find the rest of the skyjacked booty. But no more money was found, nor the remains of D B Cooper. 'That's the closest we ever got to him,' an FBI agent remarked.

And that's the way it stays. D B Cooper pulled off one of the greatest vanishing tricks in history – if he lived long enough to enjoy it.

GRAHAM STURLEY: DEATH THAT CHEATED JUSTICE

The file on Linda Sturley, missing, believed murdered, lies in a police archive marked with four words: 'File closed; suspect deceased.'

That suspect was the missing woman's husband Graham, aged 37, a former private detective who looked as if he might get away with murder – until fate played a hand. He suffered a fatal heart attack as the finger of suspicion was pointed at him.

Sturley had, said the police, the three classic attributes for carrying out a killing: motive, knowledge and opportunity. The police are certainly satisfied he did it, but the mystery of what happened to his 29-year-old pregnant wife remains.

Graham Sturley had begun an affair with his second wife Linda while he was still married to his first, Sandra. Linda was just 25 when she met Sturley in the pub one evening. They became lovers that same night, and later Sandra walked out of the marital home with their young son.

But the subsequent married life of Linda and Graham at their home, a bungalow called Irongates in Biggin Hill, Kent, was anything but made in heaven. Sturley had a penchant for extramarital affairs, and

Graham Sturley points to where the police dug up his back garden, so convinced they were that he killed his pregnant wife.

Linda was left to take solace in the arms of other men. She had a string of lovers, one of them a neighbour who worked as a dustman. Others were bus drivers, and she even taunted her husband that she was going to have another man's baby.

The last argument before her disappearance in July 1981 led to violence. Tearfully, the morning after the row, Linda told her sister that Graham had beaten and kicked her the previous evening when he raged at her that one of her lovers was the father of the child she was carrying.

Linda, a cheerful representative of the Avon cosmetics firm, vanished on 17 July 1981. For over a year, Sturley carried out a plan of deceit which fooled both his neighbours and his wife's relatives.

On the afternoon following the day she vanished, Sturley told their six-year-old daughter Sharon and son Wayne, four, that mummy wasn't coming home again. In the garden he made a bonfire of her clothes and other personal effects, and for a whole year he lived as if nothing had changed. He forged Linda's maternity benefit cheques and cheques drawn on her personal account.

He fobbed off enquiries from her mother Mrs Ada Webb, saying that her daughter was well and healthy. When her mother wanted to speak to her she was out, at the doctor's or the shops. When the time was due for the baby to be born, he telephoned her to say that his wife had walked out. He lied that she was still in touch by telephone, but wouldn't say where she was.

He did not tell them that the day after Linda's so-called 'disappearance' he was on the telephone to his own lover, Mrs Eileen Clark, inviting her to move in with him...

For a whole year – detectives were to say it was the happiest year of his life – he lived with Eileen and carried on his work as a property developer. But the bubble burst in July 1982 when, worried by Sturley's continual excuses, Mrs Webb walked into the local police station and told them the story that Sturley had spun her.

Detectives despatched to see him found him frank and willing to talk when asked about his missing wife. He said she had had numerous affairs, which she had flaunted in front of him. Later the detectives learned that the former private eye had tape recorded some of the intimate conversations between Linda and her boyfriends. The man who led the hunt for Linda, Detective Chief Inspector George Cressy, was certain Graham Sturley had murdered his wife and had spent a year hoping that his tale that she had walked out on him would be believed.

Under questioning, Sturley denied categorically that he had killed Linda. The only offence he admitted was forging the maternity benefit cheques and her personal cheques. He told detectives that she had cheated on him in the past, taking his money; he was just getting his revenge.

Hardened detective Cressy thought the alibi stank, and began a hunt for the body. The floorboards of the marital home were ripped up, the garden was dug up and surrounding woodlands were searched with dogs and heat-seeking sensors (infrared sensors can detect changes in soil temperature years after a body may have been buried). Lakes were plumbed by police divers, and forestry land as far as 48km/30 miles from the home was also searched intensively.

When police dug up the garden, Sturley said: 'I wouldn't have buried her there – it would have poisoned the flowers.'

During questioning, Sturley adopted a strange pose. He would cover his face with his hands for at least 30 seconds after each question was levelled at him – as if, before every answer, he was carefully considering what to say. The detectives who were involved were convinced they had come close to breaking him down and enticing him into making a confession. However, his nerve held, even after one marathon 16-hour interrogation session.

The family doctor told detectives that Mrs Sturley would have had to have her baby delivered by caesarean section. Her details were distributed to every hospital and clinic in Britain, but no one answering her description had given birth.

Detectives were reluctant to grill their suspect too harshly, as Sturley had a history of heart trouble and had suffered three attacks in the past. They certainly did not want him to have a fourth while he was in their custody.

But despite the lack of a body and the fact that all

evidence was purely circumstantial, George Cressy was convinced he had enough to get Graham Sturley convicted on a charge of murder. Police experts were preparing the files for prosecution on him when he dropped dead, the victim of a massive heart attack, on 6 October 1982. He was cremated a week later – and the murder file was closed once and for all, because the suspect was dead.

Afterwards George Cressy said: 'Everything we discovered and all my experience convince me of two factors... Firstly, Linda is dead. And secondly, her husband was responsible.'

NAZI TREASURE

When Adolf Hitler invaded Poland in 1939 he not only precipitated the Second World War, but he also unleashed the largest army of licensed robbers ever sanctioned by a government.

They had but one brief – to loot and plunder from vanquished countries art treasures, antiquities, gold, gems and money to provide a cultural basis for his dream of a thousand-year Reich. It all ended in less than six years. But in that time his followers amassed great fortunes, the like of which no crusade of old ever had achieved.

Even now, the mystery of the wealth the Nazis stole is a source of great contention and bitterness. In the underground vaults of Swiss banks there are said to be untold riches looted during the war. Even more of it is dispersed in South American and Arab banks, where it is used to this day by the sinister ODESSA organisation. Formed as the Third Reich was crumbling, ODESSA's aim was, and is, to protect the Nazis who escaped justice at the Nuremberg Trials. War criminals all over the world are living lives of luxury because of the greatest robbery in history, despite the tireless efforts of men such as Simon Wiesenthal to bring them to justice.

The roots of the scheme probably lay in the events of Hitler's childhood. As a teenager, he moved with his mother to the Austrian town of Linz, about 30

Inside Hermann Goering's mansion on the outskirts of Berlin hung paintings, in three and four tiers, from the plundered treasures of Europe and Russia.

km/19 miles from his birthplace at Braunau-am-Inn. When his mother died in 1908, Hitler, nurturing dreams of becoming a great artist, moved to Vienna, one of the cultural capitals of the world with its splendid galleries, museums, theatres and the opera.

Hitler tried to get into the city's Academy of Fine Arts with his portfolio of amateurish drawings. They failed to impress the selectors and they turned him down on two occasions.

Their refusal to admit him laid the basis of the simmering resentment, which he was to nurture for years. His life in Vienna became merely a painful struggle for survival; he eked out a meagre and lonely living and existed as a tramp, reduced to begging and getting his food from soup kitchens and sleeping on the streets.

By 1934, however, Adolf Hitler rose from his humble beginning to become Führer of all Germany. In the first phase of his plan to dominate Europe, he annexed Austria. Then, he knew, he would have his revenge on Vienna, the city that had treated him so badly during his formative years. He summoned the director of the provincial art museum in Linz – the town that he had left as a boy to seek fame in Vienna – Dr Karl Kerschner, and declared: 'I will make Linz the art capital of the world. It will have the finest treasures of all Europe. I will make those ungrateful peasants of Vienna feel they are living in a slum.'

He sketched out a number of designs himself, and passed them on to his personal architect, Albert Speer, ordering him to plan a museum and art gallery the like of which the world had never seen. If Speer built it, Hitler would see to it that his *Sonderauftrag Linz* (Linz Special Mission) would bring back all the treasures they could steal to this magnificent new shrine to art and culture.

That was the brief of this new Third Reich department: to plunder all they could from the subjugated lands.

Before the conquered European and Russian territories were systematically plundered by the Linz Special Mission, many treasures were stolen from Jews. Baron Louis von Rothschild, a member of the famous wine and banking dynasty and the richest man in Austria, was one of the first to be cruelly held to ransom. His mammoth art collection, containing some of the finest works by old masters, was 'acquired', together with all his assets, as the ransom Hitler demanded in return for allowing him and his family to leave Austria.

Dr Hans Posse, of the Dresden Art Museum, became Hitler's travelling expert and advised the Führer on all aspects of art. Posse bound pictures of the seized art treasures in leather volumes, which the Führer persued at his leisure. The binders themselves were later produced at Nuremberg at the end of the war as evidence of the wide-scale pilfering Hitler had sanctioned.

One by one, the territories of Europe and Russia were overrun and their bank vaults were systematically drained of gold, currency and jewellery. Special trains were commissioned to speed the treasures back to Germany, where newly constructed air-raid shelters in Munich became filled to bursting point with the plunder.

The looting spree went on for almost the whole of the war. Even in Russia, where German armies fought and died at Stalingrad and Leningrad, the art teams were busy. In 1943, two months after Hitler's most disastrous defeat of the war, when Field Marshal von Paulus surrendered 112,000 men, the robbers were still sending 60 trains, filled with stolen treasures, back to Germany each month.

Not all the loot reached its destination, however. Hermann Goering, the Luftwaffe chief, diverted vast amounts to his baronial-style mansion of Karinhall, on the outskirts of Berlin. He had so many paintings that they hung in tiers on the walls. He even proudly boasted that he sold some at a handsome profit 'because the paintings have come from the famous Goering collection'.

By early 1944 the tide of war had turned against the Germans, but still the Nazis' vast plundering went on. By then, some £17 billion of treasures had been stolen – a figure worth 30 or 40 times as much in real terms today.

Salt mines and lake bottoms were used as secret dumping grounds for much of the treasure. Some £50 million worth of gold is said to lie on the bottom of the alpine lake Toplitz to this very day. The few key men who knew the exact location are believed to have died during the final days of the war.

Shortly after the abortive attempt on Hitler's life in July 1944, eminent German industrialists held a secret meeting in Strasbourg with SS officers to secure an escape route out of Germany for the plundered loot. These men knew what Hitler refused to accept: that Germany was going to lose the war, and that the best thing to do in the circumstances was to transport the riches abroad.

It was with the money allocated at this meeting that the infamous ODESSA organisation was financed. ODESSA stands for Organisation der SS Angehorigen, or Organisation for SS members. It was amply financed and well run and at the end of the war it spirited away some of the most terrible criminals who ever lived – men with the blood of millions on their hands. Among those who escaped with ODESSA money were Adolf Eichmann, Josef Mengele, Karl Bador and Klaus Barbie. The organisation used an escape network managed by well-paid agents, and used the enormous quantities of stolen loot to finance the whole operation.

Simon Wiesenthal, a concentration camp survivor who devoted his life to tracing and bringing to justice surviving Nazi criminals, said:

'ODESSA is well run, still active, and financed largely by the stolen treasures of Europe, which Hitler plundered during the war years. The money has been used to pay for sanctuaries for war criminals, greasing the palms of corrupt government officials in those countries which give a haven to the murderers. Much of the money is probably still in Europe.'

It was to the neutral Swiss banks that the Nazis turned when their regime was nearing its end. Formerly, when the Nazis had tried to wrest from Swiss authorities details of the accounts of wealthy Jews in order to plunder them, they were furious that their requests were denied. But that self same secrecy was to provide the safest haven for their stolen riches.

In 1945 the Allies uncovered cache after cache of stolen treasures. Some of the world's greatest paintings were found crated and stored in bunkers and salt mines, which were to be their staging post en route to 'Führermuseum Linz'.

While many of the art treasures were found, intelligence experts calculate that there is still probably around £50 billion to £100 billion worth of bullion and other valuables still unaccounted for.

To give an idea of the size of these shipments, consider the find made in June 1983 in the well of a monastery in northern Italy. Workmen found the well shaft completely blocked by heavy chests filled with 60 tonnes of gold – the result of only one visit by *Sonderauftrag Linz* to the vaults of the Rome Central Bank in 1944. By 1983 that haul of gold was worth roughly £540 million, but it was only half of what was taken. ODESSA is believed to have the other half in safe keeping.

It is history's biggest robbery. Yet, apart from the

Nazis who were sentenced at Nuremberg, the majority of those responsible got away with it. They were protected both by a banking system that doesn't ask many questions and by corrupt politicians who grant refuge to Nazi criminals – at a price, of course.

ROBERTO CALVI

Roberto Calvi had all the qualifications for his chosen profession. He was a financial renegade, ruthless, ever ready to break the rules and bend the law – and he enjoyed close links with the Mafia. But Calvi was no crook in the ordinary sense of the word. He was a powerful and highly respected bank boss.

His prestigious Banco Ambrosiano, of Milan, was known as 'The Priests' Bank' because of its services to the Vatican. And as its chairman, Roberto Calvi was known as 'God's Banker'.

There was little that was godly about the work of Calvi, however. Because he handled a large proportion of the Vatican's vast investments, many less-than-reputable business clients looked to his bank to gain a spurious respectability. For them, Roberto Calvi employed whatever means he could. While one section of the bank represented the interests of the Holy Father, another laundered hot money and ran phoney companies.

Little by little, Calvi made the two sides – God and Mammon – work unwittingly together. His Vatican clients needed their assets, worth billions, moved into areas where much-needed income could be created. His criminal clients also needed their money laundered into legitimate businesses. Throughout the 1970s, the church's wealth was intermingled with the profits of vice and crime to the innocent ignorance of the one and the cynical satisfaction of the other.

Roberto Calvi not only looked after the interests of wealthy clients, both crooked and clerical, but he also lined his own pockets.

The banker's big opportunity came in the late 1970s when Italy's new left–wing government introduced tight currency restrictions to halt damaging speculation against the lira and to prevent money being salted away abroad. Calvi set up his own overseas banking branches in Switzerland and in tax havens like Panama and the Bahamas.

Money was transferred to these banks from Italy as 'secured loans' to supposedly profitable foreign companies. The companies, however, were secretly owned by Calvi and the money he loaned to himself was used to buy shares... in the Banco Ambrosiano, of course.

For Calvi's money machinations to succeed, he needed the assistance – unwitting and otherwise – of three unlikely participants. Most prominent of these was the effective head of the Vatican bank, Archbishop Paul Marcinkus. The Chicago-born cleric, who also acted as the Pope's bodyguard, was answerable only to the Pope himself. Given the job of earning the church much–needed income on its assets in properties and investments, Marcinkus would tell sceptical Vatican religious leaders: 'You can't run a church on Hail Marys alone.' More importantly to the Banco Ambrosiano, he also issued temporary 'letters of comfort', guaranteeing the stability of some of Calvi's phoney foreign companies.

Archbishop Marcinkus had been introduced to Calvi by Michael Sindona, a Sicilian entrepreneur who used the Church's cover and the banker's expertise to launder the proceeds of shady business deals. Sindona, who was later jailed in the United States for a bank fraud, also introduced Calvi to his most important client of all, Licio Gelli.

Gelli, a wealthy Italian businessman with a network of powerful friends around the world, was Calvi's top contact for clearing the bank's hot money. To ensure Calvi's trust and loyalty, Gelli introduced the banker to one of the most powerful secret societies in the world – Rome's right-wing Freemason's Lodge P2. Gelli was grand master, controlling a network of fellow members in every strata of business, military, police, the judiciary and government. He enrolled Calvi into the lodge, making him swear a Masonic oath that betrayal would be punished by '...having my tongue torn out and being buried in the sand at low water's mark, or a cable length from the shore where the tide ebbs and flows.'

Calvi was soon to discover the terrible meaning of that oath.

In 1978, Banco Ambrosiano's handling of criminally-tainted accounts drew the attention of the nation's controlling body, the Bank of Italy. Calvi asked Licio Gelli, to 'influence' investigators not to look too closely at the books. Possibly due to Gelli's influence, the investigations soon petered out. Calvi was both impressed and relieved. The connections he had made within Lodge P2 had proved invaluable. They were also to prove highly dangerous.

In 1981 Milan magistrates investigating crooked deals by an Italian-American businessman uncovered links with shady financier Michael Sindona. From there the trail led to Licio Gelli. Police raided Gelli's textile factory but, having been tipped off by police contacts, he had already fled to South America. In his haste, however, he had left behind documents proving the involvement of influential Masonic members. In a safe, police found the membership list of Lodge P2 with 962 names; from crooks to police commissioners, from cabinet ministers to heads of corporations. And, of course, Roberto Calvi.

Awaiting trial in a Milan prison cell, Calvi 'sang'. He gave chapter and verse of the secret dealings between the Vatican and the Freemasons. As a reward, he was sentenced to four years' jail for currency swindles, but was freed on appeal and astonishingly welcomed back to his old job.

Now worried about all the letters of comfort he had signed for Calvi's dodgy deals, Archbishop Paul Marcinkus intervened. He asked the Banco Ambrosiano to hand over the books of some of the foreign companies which Calvi had set up to launder money. But Calvi's foreign currency dealings were anything up to two million dollars adrift.

Calvi worked furiously to cover up his tracks and

dreamed up wild schemes to try to replace the missing money. He pleaded with Archbishop Marcinkus to extend the guarantees or to help repay some of the debts. But by now Marcinkus had run out of patience with his friend. He turned his pleas down flat and called in the debts.

In May 1982, Calvi had a secret meeting with his lawyers. He told them that he had channelled $50 million to the outlawed Polish trade union movement Solidarity, a cause close to the heart of Pope John Paul II. He also claimed he had provided the Freemason's Lodge P2 with funds to bribe leading political figures throughout Italy and Europe. In a statement that Calvi hoped would never need to be made public, he warned: 'A lot of people have a lot to answer for. If the whole thing comes out it will be enough to start World War III.'

That same month, Calvi flew in to London's Heathrow Airport on a false passport. For three weeks, the diminutive, 62-year-old banker hid away in a flat in Chelsea, rented under an assumed name. It was believed that he was attempting to contact freemasonry friends in England who could help him find a new identity abroad.

Perhaps while lying low in England he had time to study the origins of the masons in England. Did he ever liken their historical rituals to those of a band of black–cloaked English monks who gave their name to Blackfriars Bridge in the heart of London? Did he ever wonder whether those rituals were still enacted?

On 17 June he disappeared from his Chelsea hideout. The following morning he was found hanging under Blackfriars Bridge in the City of London, his body weighted with bricks.

An inquest at first decided that Calvi had committed suicide. Then doubts were raised and at a reconvened hearing the coroner revised this to an inconclusive open verdict. The jury could not decide with any certainty who had taken the banker's life.

The answer, however, was not difficult for those in the Freemason's movement back in Rome. Calvi had broken his word by informing on fellow members. It was clear to them why he had been found beneath the Blackfriars Bridge, with its ancient religious connotations, and why he had been suspended '...a cable length from the shore where the tide ebbs and flows'.

If Calvi had not squealed, he could have ended up the richest crook in Christendom. Instead, unknown killers called in the biggest IOU of all against the man known as God's Banker.

THOMPSON-BYWATERS

The case seemed cut and dried and yet Edith Thompson's final futile cries of 'Oh God, I am not guilty', as the judge pronounced the death sentence upon her, continue to echo ominously through criminal history.

Edith Thompson transgressed in the same way that millions of people around the world do every day... she had an illicit affair. Perhaps the attraction was the excitement that lifted her from a routine, humdrum life. Maybe it was sexual chemistry, which could not be denied or resisted. Whatever it was, she went to the gallows because of it, condemned as the accomplice to the murder of her husband by her enraged lover. And it was her own hand that wrote the death sentence – in scores of letters to her lover, which poured out dark and sinister plots against the man she married.

Did Edith Thompson deserve to hang? Read the following facts, then you be the jury in this compelling murder mystery.

Edith married Percy Thompson in February 1915. Percy was a shipping clerk, deemed unfit for front-line service in the First World War; she was a bookkeeper at a millinery firm. They lived together in suburban bliss in Ilford, Essex, on the fringes of London and beyond the squalor of the East End.

By all accounts, their neighbours thought them a perfectly normal couple. She was 21 when they wed and was described as a happy bride, determined to make a life with Percy. There was no strong maternal yearning for children; she explained to relatives that making a career for herself and planning a sound financial future were the primary goals.

Chance or fate threw together Edith Thompson and Frederick Bywaters in the summer of 1921. The Thompsons had gone to the Isle of Wight for the traditional August bank holiday break. They went with a party of people whose number included Bywaters, a 19-year-old employee of the Pacific and Orient Shipping Line.

Bywaters was a domineering, self-assured young man who was captivated by the older woman – and the feeling was immediately returned. She was later to admit that all the feeling prevalent in the age – that this sort of thing was wrong, that no good would come of it – disappeared during the week-long break. They did not share a bed then, but the seeds of the illicit relationship were formed and the first step taken on the pathway to the ultimate tragedy.

Avis Graydon, Edith's unmarried sister, was on the trip, and she was the only person to whom Edith confessed her new feelings. She said her marriage had degenerated into bickering and spiteful rows and she found it hard to feel any love for her husband. But this new boy... she delighted in his youthful good looks, dark wavy hair and smart appearance. Avis, with a sense of foreboding, warned her sister to be extremely careful.

In a bizarre twist, Edith managed to persuade her husband to let Frederick move into their home as a lodger. She said they could do with the extra money. But their planned adulterous affair was soon exposed when Bywaters could no longer restrain himself and told Thompson that he loved his wife. He asked poor Percy to divorce her so that she would be free to marry him. Percy refused and, after a bitter quarrel, Bywaters was thrown out of the house.

This did not spell the end of the affair. Bywaters worked aboard the vessel *SS Morea* as a laundry steward and consequently was away for long periods. He and Edith snatched brief moments of passion together at guest houses and cheap hotels. And they fuelled their desire with letters.

They were, on the face of it, damning documents. Sixty-two of them were submitted by the prosecution at the trial she was eventually to face. In them, she referred to Bywaters as 'darlint' (her pet name for him, a diminutive of darlingest). She also told how she was trying to kill her husband.

She spoke about how she was putting glass into his food: 'Big pieces too, not powdered.' She spoke of poison: 'He puts great stress on the tea tasting bitter.' And more: 'I am going to try the glass again when it is safe.' She also sent Bywaters lurid snippets from penny journals and from the *News of the World* about poison cases.

In one particularly passionate letter Edith wrote: 'This thing that I am going to do for both of us – will

183

it ever, at all, make any difference darlint? Do you understand what I mean? Will you ever think any the less of me?'

The truth, however, was that neither the glass nor the poison with which she contemplated killing her husband ever got rid of him. And the simple reason is that she administered nothing harmful to him whatsoever. The letters, experts now conclude, were the excitable love notes of a woman stimulated by an illicit affair, who worked out her passion – and proved her loyalty to her lover – with fantastic notions. With these crazy schemes, she was doing no more than binding herself to a carefree young man who roamed the world on the high seas.

In September 1922 her lover's ship docked in England. On the afternoon of 3 October, Bywaters and Edith had a secret rendezvous in a London tea shop. Later that night Edith and her husband went to the theatre in London and returned late to Ilford. As they walked to their home from the station, an assailant leaped from the darkness. It was Bywaters.

As the young man plunged a knife repeatedly into Percy, Edith screamed and cried for help, pleading with her lover: 'Oh don't, oh don't!' Edith's reaction was, said witnesses at her trial, one of genuine horror. She pleaded with a doctor who rushed to the scene to save her husband's life.

She did not tell the police that she knew the identity of the attacker, but enquiries among neighbours soon unearthed the connection. The lovers were arrested, letters seized and a trial fixed for the Old Bailey – he on a murder charge, she accused of inciting the crime.

At their trial, the prosecution alleged that the murder had been planned that very afternoon at the tea shop rendezvous. Bywaters denied this. He said an argument had ensued when he confronted Percy over his love for the man's wife, and that Percy had threatened to shoot him. 'I did not intend to kill him,' he said. 'I only meant to injure him.'

Of Edith and the love letters, he said she had a 'vivid imagination' and that she had been reading too many books. There was no plot to murder, he insisted. There was no scheme; it was a killing carried out in the heat of the moment. There was no one else the crown should look to punish, he said.

All the damaging passages in the letters were read out in court, and Edith was forced to face skilled – and often savage – cross-examination.

One of the letters referred to an abortion, which Edith had procured when she found she was carrying Bywaters's baby. Such was the high moral code of the age (and the ignorance of the jurors about such matters) that several phrases in the letter referring to the terminated pregnancy were misconstrued as being further death threats towards her husband.

Edith Thompson's barrister had to restrain himself from intervening to clear up the jurors' misunderstandings. He felt he dared not risk losing further jury sympathy for a woman who had not only cheated on her husband, but who had also had her lover's child aborted. Her lawyer's case rested on the one hard fact in her defence: the pathologist's report, which stated that no glass or poison traces had been found inside the body of Percy Thompson.

There was to be no mercy, however. A million young men of the British Empire had died in the First World War for all that was good and true – and the values for which they perished were being desperately clung to by society. The judge, Mr Justice Shearman, took pleasure in detailing Edith's 'wicked affection' for her lover. He said: 'This is a squalid and rather indecent case of lust and adultery.'

The jury took two hours to consider their verdicts. The lovers were pronounced guilty and the judge sentenced them to hang. They died on the gallows on the morning of 9 January 1923.

To the end, Frederick Bywaters remained dignified. From his condemned cell, he wrote in defence of his lover: 'For her to be hanged as a criminal is too awful. She didn't commit the murder. I did. She never planned it, she never knew about it. She is innocent, absolutely innocent.'

What is your verdict?

BLACK DAHLIA: ELIZABETH SHORT

It was one of the goriest sights even hardened Los Angeles cops had ever encountered. The corpse of a young woman, lying in a scrub on a vacant lot on 15 January 1947, had been hideously mutilated. The woman had been dead for five days before her remains were spotted on the building site on South Norton Avenue by a young mother and her five-year-old daughter. They did not know what the object was until they were almost on top of it. For the torso had been cut completely in half at the waist.

The victim had been tortured for about three days. Rope burns revealed that she had been hung upside down by her wrists and ankles. She had been burned with cigarettes. Slow and careful knife incisions had been made all over her body while she was still alive. Her breasts had been particularly mutilated and her throat had been slit from ear to ear. After the poor girl had eventually died, the killer had drained her body of every drop of blood, had bisected it and then washed the two parts. He had even shampooed her hair and hennaed it.

In one particular act of savagery, the butcher had gouged a rose tattoo out of one thigh and had carved into the other one the initials 'BD'. They gave the first clue to the identity of the raven-haired beauty so

Would-be actress Elizabeth Anne Short, nicknamed the Black Dahlia, was found dead on a vacant lot. Her awful murder even shocked the hardened LA cops.

brutally slaughtered. For they stood for Black Dahlia – the nickname of the 22-year-old would-be actress, Elizabeth Anne Short.

Elizabeth was just like the hundreds of other young girls who had found their way to Los Angeles, lured by the sunshine and the notion of Hollywood fame and fortune. Born one of four sisters near Salem, Massachusetts, her family moved to Boston, from where she ran away. She worked as a waitress in Miami and in a bar in Chicago before finding her way to Santa Barbara, California.

There she was picked up for under-age drinking and shipped back East. On the way, she jumped train and made her way back to the West Coast, where she queued for bit-part acting jobs. The nearest she came to breaking into the movies was working as an usherette. Like many aspiring actresses before her, she ended up supplementing her wages by using her body as a meal ticket.

In what could have been the luckiest break of her brief life, Elizabeth met US Air Force Major Matthew Gordon Jr and the pair fell in love. It could have been the luckiest break in her life – but the major died in an air crash just after the Second World War ended. It is likely that the couple were engaged; certainly his mother sent Elizabeth a letter of condolence from the family home in Pueblo, Colorado.

Gordon's death sent Elizabeth Short into a downhill spiral. She began drinking heavily and embarked on a string of affairs. She worked as a waitress by day and haunted sleazy bars by night. Little by little, she began accepting money for her favours – and revelled in the nickname Black Dahlia, given to her by her boyfriends who admired her slinky black apparel.

Poor Elizabeth (or Beth as she now usually called herself) got one more chance of breaking out of the spiral of sleaze and vice. She received another proposal of marriage and is believed to have accepted. Tragically, this suitor also died.

The last known address of Beth Short was in San Diego, where she had ended up after a chance meeting with a woman at a movie theatre. The woman befriended her, took pity on her and allowed her to share her home after Short had given her a hard-luck story of a dead husband and a lost baby.

In San Diego, Beth met a salesman named Robert 'Red' Manley who, just a week before her death, gave her a lift back to Los Angeles. Manley dropped her off at the Biltmore Hotel, the doorman clearly recalling that she had dawdled around the lobby for three hours waiting for someone who never turned up. Over the next few days she bumped into several of her old bar-room friends, but she was always alone. She seemed, they said, to be afraid of someone.

The last sighting of the Black Dahlia was on 10 January. When her butchered body was discovered five days later, the police already had her prints on their files because of the under-age drinking offence years before in Santa Barbara. They knew who she was, but they had no clues whatsoever as to her killer.

On 24 January 1947 a Los Angeles newspaper received a package containing Elizabeth Short's birth certificate, social security card and an address book with most of the pages ripped out. A message stuck together from press headlines read: 'HERE ARE DAHLIA'S BELONGINGS. LETTER TO FOLLOW.'

A second note arrived on 27 January: 'TURNING IN WED JAN 29, 10 am. HAD MY FUN AT POLICE – BLACK DAHLIA AVENGER.'

A third note arrived on 29 January: 'HAVE CHANGED MY MIND. YOU WOULD NOT GIVE ME A SQUARE DEAL. DAHLIA KILLING WAS JUSTIFIED.'

That was the final note; after that, the trail again went cold.

Manley, the number one suspect at the start of the murder hunt, was finally but firmly cleared by detectives. He told police that on the journey from San Diego to Los Angeles he had asked Elizabeth about deep scratch marks on her arms. She told him that they were inflicted by a jealous boyfriend.

The most intriguing theory propounded by the Los Angeles Police Department was that Elizabeth Short was murdered by a woman. Captain Donohoe, in charge of the investigation, said he believed this to be the case because of the nature of the injuries and the spite with which they were inflicted. There was some evidence that Elizabeth had been involved in a lesbian relationship, but had broken it off shortly before the killing. A 'repulsed lesbian' became the phrase used on the unclosed police files.

Unusually, for a single slaying in violent Los Angeles, the savage slaughter of the Black Dahlia struck a chord with an angry and frightened public. The striking photographs of the dark beauty in the newspapers contrasted starkly with the grisly scene on the empty lot. The stories of torture were the stuff nightmares – and Hollywood horror movies – were made of. Beth's death incited an astonishing number of false reports and even false confessions. In all, 50 men claimed to have been the killer, but not one of them could conceivably have committed the crime.